Play has been associated with early childhood, but there's a shift towards understanding its positive impact on teenagers' learning, health, and overall wellbeing. We are seeing a change in societal attitudes and this book is highly relevant.

Sarah Watkins, *Lecturer and Author*

Play and Adolescence

Play provides us with the autonomy to test out our ideas, experience appropriate risks, and build relationships. In *Play and Adolescence*, Fey Cole explores how those working with teenagers can meaningfully incorporate play into the learning environment, demonstrating its critical contribution to cognitive development, emotional resilience, and social connection in this pivotal life stage.

Drawing on interdisciplinary research and international practice, this accessible and insightful book examines play across diverse settings—from formal classrooms to community spaces and digital environments. Through real-life experiences and case studies from across the globe, readers discover how playful learning fosters teenagers' sense of belonging while enhancing critical thinking and creativity. The book addresses cultural, structural, and policy-related barriers to play while offering actionable strategies for implementation.

This resource will particularly benefit those working in education, youth services, and community development. It serves as both a resource tool and source of evidence-based effective practice for anyone committed to creating more dynamic, inclusive learning environments that prepare adolescents for future success through purposeful play.

Fey Cole is a Lecturer in Further and Higher Education and a Teaching and Learning Advisor in the UK.

Play and Adolescence

Developing a Playful Pedagogical Approach for Teenagers' Holistic Learning, Growth, and Wellbeing

Fey Cole

LONDON AND NEW YORK

Designed cover image: © Getty Images

First published 2026
by Routledge
4 Park Square, Milton Park, Abingdon, Oxon OX14 4RN

and by Routledge
605 Third Avenue, New York, NY 10158

Routledge is an imprint of the Taylor & Francis Group, an informa business

© 2026 Fey Cole

The right of Fey Cole to be identified as author of this work has been asserted in accordance with sections 77 and 78 of the Copyright, Designs and Patents Act 1988.

All rights reserved. No part of this book may be reprinted or reproduced or utilised in any form or by any electronic, mechanical, or other means, now known or hereafter invented, including photocopying and recording, or in any information storage or retrieval system, without permission in writing from the publishers.

Trademark notice: Product or corporate names may be trademarks or registered trademarks, and are used only for identification and explanation without intent to infringe.

British Library Cataloguing-in-Publication Data
A catalogue record for this book is available from the British Library

ISBN: 978-1-032-91282-0 (hbk)
ISBN: 978-1-032-91281-3 (pbk)
ISBN: 978-1-003-56236-8 (ebk)

DOI: 10.4324/9781003562368

Typeset in Galliard
by SPi Technologies India Pvt Ltd (Straive)

Contents

Acknowledgements	ix
Introduction	1
1 Play in the teenage years	5
2 Gaining a sense of belonging and identity through play	17
3 Developing playful skills for future success	23
4 The benefits of play for emotional health and wellbeing	30
5 Challenging assumptions of play	38
6 Taking a risk: Physically and mentally	46
7 Never too old to play: Being a role model and advocate of play	57
8 Do we grow out of play or is it taken from us?	64
9 The seriousness of play	71
10 Play in the classroom	78
11 Using play to engage with the wider community	84
12 Using technology to play and prosper	92

13 True play: Understanding the difference of play in and out of the classroom — 101

14 Play at breaktimes — 112

15 Play after school — 120

16 Developing a lifetime commitment to play — 125

   Conclusion — 132

   Index — *135*

Acknowledgements

The subject of this book leads me to reflect on the playful adolescent members of the family. Ruby, Matilda, Henry, Indiana, and Carter: thank you for being an inspiration to my research. The memories I have of time with you all make me grin, and it is a joy to have so many happy times together. To know that no matter how old any of us gets, I know our future will include lots of play, laughter, and love. Not only does your energy bring a lot of happiness, but you do the same for the people around us, whether that be friends or a stranger passing by. You are the essence of what a community needs more of. Proud to be Mummy and Auntie to you absolute legends.

To my Mum, Fiona Johnstone-Clark – for many years it was you and I. I am grateful for all the love, support, guidance, and wisdom you have given me which has led me here. The way you proofread my work is a reminder of your attentiveness and desire to make sure everything is just right for us. I noticed a comma in Ruby's dissertation that could only be you. Thank you for all you do behind the scenes for us.

I would like to thank everyone who engaged with my questionnaires, interviews, and discussions. Without you, my insight into this area would not have been enriched. I have the utmost respect for all those advocating the Right to Play. Many thanks to my editor, Alison Foyle, and the team at Routledge for their support and for making this book a reality.

At the year of writing this book, PlayBoard, the lead organisation for Play in Northern Ireland, becomes forty. I have also had the fortieth milestone this year and am in awe that the organisation has been championing play for my entire lifetime. I am very proud to be a Director of PlayBoard as part of the Executive Committee and look forward to seeing what comes next for the organisation. Thank you for having me as part of the play journey. Huge appreciation to the champions involved in the organisation over the past forty years and to those who progress the agenda forward.

When coming to the end of this book, I felt like I had a month of play. The Early Years team at the College championed the power of play at our annual conference, strategic plans were made through Lego Serious Play, I took a role in a family business to advocate for community play, I was asked to speak at two future play conferences, and I gained a monster of a bruise on my shin from tumbling over a hedgerow during family time. It was a beautiful conclusion to inspire me to maintain the drive of completing this book, and I thank all the playful people around me who keep my play energy up and remind me why it is so vital for emotional wellbeing and adult life.

To the community around me, thank you. It is important to me that we continue to showcase the wonderful work that happens in Northern Ireland. We might be small, but we are mighty. In this past month, our local football club won the Irish League for the first time, and with this falling over a bank holiday, all the community came out to play. As we celebrated, I enjoyed being with the different generations of our family and friends, past and current students, strangers who became friends. The people of the town of Dungannon were a fabulous reminder of how much good we have surrounding us. Sport and play connect all generations and build community.

Since 2020, I have undertaken a lot of reflective analysis on values-based practice. I have homed in on what guides my approach and strive to ensure that four values underpin all I do: kindness, play, curiosity, and community. This year I was bestowed an Honorary Professorship from Hubei University in China for my support for international teacher education. What meant so much to me was that kindness was also instrumental in my receiving of this honour. Hard work can get you far, hard work without kindness is worthless. I would like to thank the Confucius Institute for welcoming me as part of the global family and being the reminder that what unites us is friendship, care, and appreciation for one another.

I draw the acknowledgements to a close knowing there are many other people who have led me to the creation of this book. My darling husband, Richard Cole, you really are the most playful of us all. Thank you for being you. Thank you for running with my barrage of ideas, and thank you for the spontaneity that ensures that life is filled with happiness. I come back to Ruby, Matilda, and Henry – it is fun being Mum to adolescents. Keep saying out loud what is in your head, remember to mix things up, and tell the universe what you want it to bring you. It will come. I also want to thank my mother-in-law, Elizabeth Cotterell, who is always there when we need her. The endless supply of biscuits whilst we all enjoy each other's company reminds us how loved we are.

And finally, to you dear reader. You have picked up this book because you are curious. You are interested in play. You may already be a huge champion of play. I am glad you are here. Read a chapter, make a plan. Maybe after that, go climb a tree, draw a doodle, dig out a pack of cards. Your leadership and role-modelling will inspire others.

Introduction

I write this introduction on the 3rd of January, the night before returning to routine after a break where all the household have switched off and we have been able to be fully present with one another. The time has gone quickly, but my brain is pinging with exciting ideas for new things I can do to bring some more joy into the schedule, both at work and at home. Prior to the holidays, my brain was not engaging to this same extent. As my mind wanders, I am reminded of Mihaly Csikszentmihalyi's (1990) theory of *flow*, which was inspired by his observations of artists fully immersed in their work, where they were completely focussed on the one thing in front of them. His theory led to his being viewed as a pioneer for the next generation of psychologists researching the study of happiness, and Csikszentmihalyi stressed that happiness was not something we find through external objects but a feeling gained from how we invest in our own psychic energy. We will explore his theory of flow in Chapter 9 and how flow and play can be seen as interlinked, but what is relevant here is the importance of providing our brains with space to lose ourselves and not be distracted by the numerous factors that bombard us throughout our daily schedule.

Csikszentmihalyi (1990) wrote, "Contrary to what we tend to assume, the normal state of the mind is chaos…when we are left alone, with no demands on attention, the basic order of the mind reveals itself". By slowing down and finding peace, we provide ourselves with the space to reflect on what we want to focus on and come up with new ideas and opportunities. As you read this book, there is no need to rush. Give yourself the space to reflect, doodle, talk with others, and return back and forth as suits your creative mind. This book is aimed as a catalyst to support those already doing amazing things, to explore how play can be embedded into schedules so that when we work with young people in their teenage years, they can find their own flow, strengthen their confidence, and gain playful strategies to support them in their holistic wellbeing and development. As I often tell my own children, 'We need to slow down, to go quicker'; giving ourselves time to be immersed in the moment sharpens our focus and provides us with space to think things through with a stronger clarity.

DOI: 10.4324/9781003562368-1

Each chapter of this book is informed by educators and professionals working with young people and draws on my own research and my experiences of working with young people in their adolescent years. Having begun my career in the field of Early Years, I continued my professional development by training as a Playworker, before moving into lecturing at a Further and Higher Education College. My time as a Playworker has been influential in my professional values and approach when working with young people, and it led to my exploration of how play can be used as a tool to support all areas of our lives, from learning to feeling good about ourselves.

For any Playworkers reading, I believe you will understand when I write that when you are in a room of adults who are committed to play, life feels better. You smile more, you learn more, you appreciate more. My favourite professional get-togethers are ones with a play focus. There is always a feeling of wonder and awe that impacts every aspect of the event. This book comes from many years of learning how to articulate the power and seriousness of play and from researching its benefits for young people once they transition from the period of childhood, where play is seen as acceptable, to a new phase of life. I write acceptable, as even in children's early years, I see first-hand how much we in the Early Years and Primary School Aged Sector have to push and champion the importance of play for children's learning, development, and wellbeing. Chapter 1 in this book will explore how play may look in the teenage years and introduce you to pedagogical approaches that embrace play for learning once we move out of the phase of life that is traditionally associated with being playful. It will also investigate how play benefits the individual once they progress into adulthood.

As you move into Chapter 2, the impact of play for teenagers' holistic growth and wellbeing is explored further, evaluating how it helps to develop a sense of belonging and how play can be used to develop inclusive and stimulating environments. Chapter 3 reviews trends in future job opportunities and how play is incorporated into the skills needed for the workforce in a variety of different sectors. Work life has progressed dramatically over the last century, and young people require skills unlike those of their parents or grandparents' generations. In Chapter 4, the focus is on wellbeing and how play can be a factor for young people feeling healthier, happier, and more content with life. For any of us working with children and young people, the mental health crisis is a frightening epidemic that is influencing our approach, and we need to build on the services and support we offer, so that we can implement a collaborative approach to support young people and provide them with the strategies to understand their emotions effectively and feel able to express these effectively.

In Chapter 5, we will challenge the assumptions of play and evaluate how play is approached differently in the adolescent years. In these years, it can be complicated for young people to stand out from the crowd and fully embrace who they are, so that chapter reviews strategies as to how teenagers can explore their own identities, skills, and interests through safe, playful mechanisms. The next chapter, Chapter 6, reminds us of the importance of young people being active and gaining opportunities to connect with the natural world. Risky play can provide positive mental and physical challenges that enhance good endorphins and stimulation, providing young people the opportunity to experiment with risk in a safe and affirmative environment.

Chapter 7 is a call to action to you, the reader. Role modelling is a crucial component for integrating play, and this chapter encourages you to evaluate your relationship with play and how play builds a positive culture for all within the educational environment. This leads us to Chapter 8, where our relationship with play is explored further and we gain some insight into how play looks around the globe throughout different stages of life. In Chapter 9, the seriousness of play is analysed in detail, exploring how play can lead to positive educational outcomes.

For those working in the classroom, Chapter 10 draws on case studies demonstrating how play has been incorporated into the learning environment. These interviews with professionals will support you in embedding your own playful pedagogical approaches that draw on the previous chapters. Frequently, we see young people in their adolescent years sitting on the outskirts of society, feeling disengaged from their local community. In Chapter 11, strategies for using play to engage young people with their community are reviewed, alongside teenagers' own experiences of these types of playful opportunities. Technology is continually evolving and is integrated into all our lives. With this in mind, Chapter 12 reviews how we as adults can embrace technology for playful learning strategies that build on young people's interests and skills.

Within this book, the primary focus is on playful approaches for the educational environment. As a Playworker, I am very aware that this can move away from play in its true and raw essence. In Chapter 13, case studies from Youth Workers and Playworkers are shared to explore the benefits of true play for young people in their adolescent years. True play and play-based approaches are explored further through case studies in Chapters 14 and 15, to provide you with ideas for enhancing teenagers' breaks and after-school/college activities through playful mechanisms. The final chapter of the book further delves into how play supports us throughout our lives and its value for overcoming obstacles and setbacks.

The day before I wrote this introduction and started to explore in detail how my research could be presented to you, I woke up with my shoulders stiff. On inspection, I realised I had some significant bruising under each of my arms. There was no need to panic on this finding, all is still well, and once I woke up properly, I had a good chuckle to myself as it dawned on me what I had done to myself. Whilst I promote play for all ages, I decided, on the first day of the new year, I still had the physical strength of a ten-year-old at play and fell off a tyre climbing wall that our family were hanging off as part of a New Year's holiday day out. Grabbing a climbing rope as I went, I found myself sliding down it onto a well-padded floor. It was the best fun, and when I say I live my values, I mean it. Play is incorporated into everyday life. Although the rope burn is unfortunate on both my arms, I am experienced enough at play to know how to fall safely, and although I took some risk, the laughter and interactions that came from the experience are what I take from the day trip, and this risk can very much be seen as healthy. The unusual bruising was a little less appreciated but brought good-humoured laughter from the family when I showed them what the climbing wall had resulted in for me.

As we get older, we become more and more bubble-wrapped. I am happy to be challenged on this statement, but I ask you: when did you last climb over a fence or play a physically strenuous game for no purpose? Of course, safety must be prioritised, but healthy risk is part of life and brings with it some freedom to let go of tension and stress. Every school holiday, I return to work with child-like shin bruises from climbing a tree or bumping down a hill, and they are part of childhood that I am quite content to keep. Cast your mind back to childhood. Is there a minimal bruise or graze that you remember from play? I'm not talking about sad moments, where people were unkind or when you bumped into something accidentally, but a time when you were fully immersed in play. I am going to take the odds that you remember that moment with fondness. Your friends might even have been impressed when you showed them once they knew you were ok. There is a freedom we lose when we 'grow out' of physical play, and that freedom also provides us with the opportunities to test and challenge ourselves and overcome barriers – essential skills not just for teenage years but for life. Of course, not all play is rough and tumble. It does not have to be, and we will explore this further in the book, hopefully challenging your own perceptions of what play is and delving into ways we can capture the joy and learning that come from adopting playful approaches to education.

Reference

Csikszentmihalyi, M. (1990) *Flow: The Psychology of Optimal Experience*. New York: Harper and Row.

Chapter 1

Play in the teenage years

What is childhood? I get to ask this question to students at the start of the academic year when teaching a unit on the social construction of childhood, and we unravel it as the term progresses. We have not come up with a fully comprehensive answer yet, but there is a lot of fun and learning as we probe and unpick this question in detail.

I took to social media with a questionnaire to find out others' perspectives, and I have included some examples of the answers provided. The answers below do not come from those studying this subject or working as educators. The responses were interesting and give some indication that a definitive answer can be complicated.

After I put together the social media questionnaire, I texted my 21-year-old, who was out at a restaurant with a group of five friends around the same age. They are all at university together and live away from their hometowns, in the second and third year of their chosen courses, so have lived away from home for some time now. I tapped out on my phone 'Are you an adult?' She immediately replied, 'No'. A few minutes later, the question must have been asked around the table as I got a second reply, 'We have decided that we are adults in life, but children at heart'. (At this point, it's probably worth sharing that our family frequently text each other random questions that have no context, hence her speedy reply and further consideration!) I did leave her to enjoy the meal after this but followed on with a discussion later in the week, to hear why that had been their conclusion. I predicted that when I asked adults when they felt they became an adult, they would respond with still feeling a child in some ways. This was the response from this group of young adults. Studying, cooking, working, and making decisions were all linked to adulthood, whereas going out, games nights, friendships, and silliness were associated with childhood. At my daughter's current age, I was her Mum. I believe that this probably made me see myself as more 'adult' than she sees herself, but I still see myself with 'child-like' qualities now. In 1918, the Fisher Act made secondary school education compulsory for females up to the age of 14, which would leave women of that generation leaving school seven years before their 21st birthday. I am sure their opinion would differ again. I also acknowledge that my social media

DOI: 10.4324/9781003562368-2

questionnaire is shared with mainly Western perspectives. The answers to what initially seem like three simple questions show that being an adolescent is complex and confusing, not just for the individual but also for the wider society.

Question 1: What is the difference between childhood and adulthood?

Rose's eight-year-old daughter

When you're young, you get to play, and grown-ups do all the boring stuff like cleaning and working. I don't have to worry about anything, but adults are always busy and sometimes tired. I think childhood is about having fun, and being an adult is about doing jobs.

Liam, age 16

The difference is that children don't have to think about big responsibilities, like paying for things or planning for the future. Adults have to figure everything out on their own. As a teenager, I'm kind of in the middle because I'm learning to take responsibility, but I still get some help.

Margaret, age 72

Childhood is a time to learn and enjoy yourself, while adulthood is about taking care of yourself and others. As a child, you depend on people to guide you, but as an adult, people depend on you. It's a big shift, but it happens gradually.

A common theme in the responses was the responsibilities that came with adulthood, from both working and caring for others. There was no discussion of play in the adult years in the answers provided.

Question 2: Is there a difference between childhood and adolescence? (Children/teenagers)

Thirteen-year-old female

When I was little, everything was easy because adults made all the decisions. Now that I'm a teenager, I have to figure out who I am, deal with school stress, and my parents can decide if they don't want me to do something. But at least I can hang out with my friends without my mum watching me all the time.

Jason, age 40

When I think about being a child, it was all about playing and being carefree. As a teenager, I started wanting independence, but I also felt a lot of pressure from school and figuring out my future. Looking back, being a child felt simpler, while being a teenager was more about testing boundaries.

Elena, age 32

> For me, being a child was about having fun and being close to my family. As a teenager, I remember feeling torn between wanting to grow up fast and still wanting my parents' support. It was exciting but also stressful because I started caring about how I looked and what others thought of me.

Childhood and adolescence felt like a grey area, in how people responded. Adolescence can often feel like a transitional period, leaving it even more difficult to feel secure and fully understand who we are and where we belong.

Question 3: At what age do we stop being children?

Sofia, age 19

> I think I stopped being a child when I moved away for university. Living on my own, managing my budget, and making decisions about my future made me grow up quickly. Even though I still call my parents for advice, I feel more like an adult now.

X, 15-year-old male

> I felt like I stopped being a child when I started helping in my family's shop at 13. I couldn't just play all the time because I had responsibilities like stocking shelves and serving customers. It made me grow up faster than some of my friends.

Priya, age 25

> I stopped being a child when my family moved countries when I was 10. I had to translate for my parents, help them navigate things like doctors' appointments, and take care of my younger siblings. I grew up quickly because my family needed me to.

Within the questionnaire, information on support lines had been included, alongside information requesting that individuals not include information on past trauma, explaining the context of how information would be used. This was important, as my background gave me the insight to appreciate that many people will have lived through difficult circumstances that can lead to a feeling of having to grow up quickly. As seen from the examples above, responsibilities are again linked to being an adult. There is not a definitive age where we become adults in mindset, there are developmental milestones and legal jurisdictions, but we move through life at different rates, and the definition of each stage of life adapts with the generations.

What the conversations and questions around this area did leave me to question is why do adults often still see themselves as children but not still refer to themselves as teenagers? Is it because we still have a need to feel the security of others taking care of us, or is it because we are still playful and sometimes find ourselves struggling with the conformity that society expects from us in our teenage and adult years?

With these perspectives in mind, it can be complicated to incorporate play into routines as people move out of childhood. It is not viewed as a natural element for adolescents and adults and yet brings with it a wealth of benefits, not just for learning but for personal growth and wellbeing. Irish playwright George Bernard Shaw (Goodreads, 2025) said, "We don't stop playing because we grow old; we grow old because we stop playing." In adolescence, we can extend play so that joy and creative thinking can become embedded into daily routines as a normalised, lifelong activity that makes people feel good. If this is what it can do for us, why wouldn't we want to keep playing? What we do need to understand is how crucial it is in the adolescent years and how play can be a positive influence at this stage of development.

The development of the teenage brain

Adolescence is typically defined as the period between 12 and 19 years of age and is characterised by significant changes in both physical and psychological development; this is when the brain undergoes some of the most profound transformations in our lifetime. During the adolescent period, the teenage brain is shaped by biological, environmental, and social factors, all of which influence cognitive, emotional, and behavioural development. One of the most notable changes during adolescence is the development of grey and white matter in the brain. Grey matter, which contains most of the brain's neuronal cell bodies, increases in volume during childhood and peaks in early adolescence. However, as adolescence progresses, grey matter begins to decline through a process known as synaptic pruning. Synaptic pruning eliminates weaker synaptic connections while strengthening others, thus increasing the efficiency of the brain's neural networks (Blakemore & Mills, 2014). This pruning process is vital for cognitive development, as it allows the brain to focus on more efficient and specialised connections. White matter, which consists of myelinated axons that help transmit signals between neurons, increases steadily during adolescence. The development of white matter is important for improving the brain's communication pathways, enhancing cognitive functions such as decision-making, attention, and learning (Paus et al., 2008). As white matter increases, so does the brain's ability to process information more quickly and effectively.

During this critical developmental period, play remains an essential element for developing healthy cognitive and emotional growth. Research shows that play-based activities contribute to the development of executive functions such as planning, adaptability, and self-regulation (Diamond & Ling, 2016). These activities also support the integration of neural pathways strengthened during the maturation of white matter, allowing adolescents to apply new cognitive skills in real-world contexts (Vygotsky, 1978). Social play can enable teenagers to navigate complex social dynamics, improve communication skills, and build resilience (Pellegrini & Smith, 1998). Structured and unstructured play provides opportunities to reduce stress and anxiety as well as to explore identity and autonomy, both of which are crucial developmental tasks during adolescence (Spencer et al., 2020). Integrating play into educational and recreational routines can significantly enhance the neurological and psychological benefits of this formative stage of life.

The prefrontal cortex, located at the front of the brain, is responsible for higher-order cognitive functions such as decision-making, impulse control, and reasoning. However, this region is one of the last to fully mature, and development continues into the mid-twenties (Casey et al., 2008). During adolescence, the prefrontal cortex undergoes significant changes, including increased connectivity with other brain regions, which gradually improves cognitive control and executive functions. This delayed development of the prefrontal cortex explains why teenagers often exhibit impulsive and risk-taking behaviour. The prefrontal cortex's relative immaturity during adolescence means that the brain's cognitive control systems are not fully developed, leading to difficulties in regulating emotions and making rational decisions (Luna et al., 2015).

In situations involving heightened emotions or peer pressure, teenagers may rely more on instinctual responses from other parts of the brain, such as the limbic system, rather than the rational decision-making processes governed by the prefrontal cortex. Evidence suggests that engaging adolescents in structured play and experiential learning activities can strengthen the connections between the prefrontal cortex and other brain regions, thereby enhancing their ability to regulate emotions and make informed decisions (Crone & Dahl, 2012). By recognising the ongoing development of the prefrontal cortex, educators and practitioners can implement activities that both stimulate its growth and support teenagers in navigating the challenges of adolescence.

The limbic system, a group of structures located deep within the brain, is primarily involved in processing emotions and regulating motivation. Two key components of the limbic system, the amygdala and the nucleus accumbens, play critical roles in emotional responses and reward processing, both of which are highly active during adolescence. The limbic system matures earlier than the prefrontal cortex, which leads to an imbalance between emotional and cognitive control during adolescence (Steinberg, 2014). The amygdala is particularly important for processing emotions, especially fear and aggression. Research shows that, during adolescence, the amygdala becomes more sensitive to emotional stimuli, which can lead to heightened emotional responses in teenagers (Burnett et al., 2011). This increased emotional reactivity is often coupled with reduced emotional regulation due to the underdeveloped prefrontal cortex, making teenagers more prone to mood swings, impulsivity, and risky behaviour. The nucleus accumbens, another component of the limbic system, is central to the brain's reward circuitry. During adolescence, this region becomes hypersensitive to rewards, which can lead to increased risk-taking behaviour. Teenagers are more likely to engage in activities that provide immediate rewards, such as trying new experiences or seeking social approval, even if these behaviours carry potential risks (Galván, 2010). The heightened reward sensitivity in adolescence is believed to be adaptive, encouraging teenagers to explore new environments and seek independence from their parents, and both activities are important for the transition to adulthood.

Given the heightened emotional reactivity and reward sensitivity during adolescence, play is a crucial mechanism for developing emotional regulation and adaptive behaviours. Panksepp's (2007) research found that engaging in playful interactions can help balance the activity of the limbic system by providing structured opportunities for positive emotional experiences and safe exploration of novelty (Panksepp, 2007). Play promotes the development of neural pathways associated with emotional resilience and cognitive flexibility, facilitating the integration of emotional and executive functions (Elkind, 2007). Play has been shown to moderate the influence of heightened reward sensitivity by offering opportunities for intrinsic motivation and self-directed learning, which can mitigate impulsivity and risk-taking behaviours (Howard-Jones, 2016). By supporting the dynamic interaction between the prefrontal cortex and the limbic system, play can be a beneficial tool to develop the emotional and cognitive skills that adolescents need to navigate the challenges of this developmental stage effectively.

Neuroplasticity in the teenage brain

Adolescence is a period of heightened neuroplasticity, meaning that the brain is particularly malleable and responsive to environmental influences. Neuroplasticity allows the teenage brain to adapt and reorganise itself in response to new experiences, making adolescence a crucial period for learning and skill development (Blakemore & Choudhury, 2006). However, this heightened plasticity also means that the teenage brain is more vulnerable to negative influences, such as stress or trauma. Positive experiences, such as education, social interactions, and physical activity, can enhance the development of the teenage brain by promoting healthy synaptic connections and reinforcing adaptive behaviours. Conversely, exposure to adverse environments can disrupt brain development and lead to long-term cognitive and emotional challenges. For example, research has shown that chronic stress during adolescence can impair the functioning of the prefrontal cortex and hippocampus, leading to difficulties in memory, learning, and emotional regulation (Romeo, 2017). The heightened neuroplasticity of the teenage brain also means that adolescence is an optimal time for interventions that promote mental health and wellbeing.

Given this neuroplasticity, play represents a particularly valuable tool for further developing resilience and supporting adaptive neural development during adolescence. Play has been shown to enhance synaptic plasticity by stimulating diverse areas of the brain, building connections between cognitive, emotional, and motor pathways (Kolb et al., 2003). It provides a safe and engaging environment for adolescents to navigate challenges, practice problem-solving, and build interpersonal skills, reinforcing positive neural adaptations (Pellegrini, 2009). Research also highlights the role of play in mitigating the effects of chronic stress, as it can reduce the overactivation of the hypothalamic-pituitary-adrenal (HPA) axis and promote the release of neurochemicals such as dopamine and serotonin, which are crucial for mood regulation and cognitive functioning (Lester & Russell, 2010). By leveraging the neuroplasticity of the teenage brain, structured and unstructured play can serve as a powerful mechanism to support emotional wellbeing, enhance learning, and prepare adolescents for the challenges that come throughout the rest of the life. As a result, young people will be able to face obstacles with a positive and healthy mindset.

Teenage play

Play during childhood typically includes imaginative, unstructured activities that promote cognitive and emotional development. In adolescence, the definition of play expands, incorporating more structured forms, including competitive sports, video games, social interactions, and creative pursuits such as music or art, something we will explore throughout the book. Adolescents still engage in leisure activities for enjoyment, but the motivations behind these activities often become more complex, influenced by social, cognitive, and emotional factors (Pellegrini, 2009). Play for teenagers could be understood

Figure 1.1 Intrinsic and extrinsic motivations. (Created by the author using Canva.)

as activities that provide pleasure, challenge, and opportunities for self-expression as well as opportunities to explore social roles, identities, and relationships (Kane, 2016). Whereas childhood play might be more solitary or centred on parental guidance, teenage play often becomes more social and peer-oriented, involving cooperative as well as competitive dynamics. Play during this time serves both intrinsic and extrinsic needs. Think back to your own teenage experiences of play; what does your mind remember? Consider the emotions that these memories bring, and I would expect that they bring a feeling of joy and nostalgia. When we reflect on our teenage years, often it is the dance routines we made up with friends (cue the Spice Girls and Backstreet Boys for me!), the football kick-abouts we had with our mates, or the journal that knew all our secrets, rather than the days spent sitting trolling over textbooks. Those moments matter and helped us to build relationships, explore what motivated us, and face challenges with laughter. We will explore intrinsic and extrinsic motivations later in the book, but use the image to consider what motivates you now and what may have motivated you in the teenage years. Consider the influence of others at both stages of life as you reflect on this.

Adolescence is marked by significant cognitive development, especially in terms of abstract thinking, problem-solving, and reasoning (Steinberg, 2014). Play in the teenage years reflects this cognitive maturation, often incorporating more complex forms of strategy, competition, and creativity. An example of this could be teenagers drawn to video games that require tactical planning or to sports that involve intricate team dynamics. These forms of play serve to stimulate the developing brain, offering adolescents opportunities to test their reasoning and decision-making skills in a low-risk environment (Granic et al., 2014). As we move into adulthood, the stakes can become higher and can prevent us from feeling able to continue to test out these skills, so it is incredibly valuable to have this opportunity in the teenage years so that, as we grow older, we feel secure to make positive choices and understand group dynamics.

Returning to the development of the adolescent brain, one of the most important contributions of play to the teenager's brain development is its influence on the prefrontal cortex, which we have recognised governs executive functions such as decision-making, impulse control, and planning. Play, especially games that require strategic thinking and problem-solving, can help strengthen neural pathways in the prefrontal cortex. Blakemore and Mills (2014) found that adolescents who engage in cognitively demanding play, such as video games or complex sports, demonstrate improved executive functioning, which is critical during a time when the prefrontal cortex is still maturing. Play contributes to emotional regulation by engaging the limbic system, particularly the amygdala, which is responsible for processing emotions. Physical play, such as sports, allows teenagers to release stress and regulate emotions through physical exertion, whereas creative play, such as art or music, provides an outlet for emotional expression.

Regular engagement in these types of play helps adolescents develop coping mechanisms and emotional intelligence, which are essential for navigating the emotional challenges of adolescence (Sutton-Smith, 2008). Play also enhances social cognition by providing space to explore interpersonal interactions and cooperation, which are crucial for adolescent development. Games and sports that involve teamwork and competition help teenagers learn to navigate social dynamics, resolve conflicts, and build relationships. These social aspects of play stimulate the development of neural circuits in the brain that are associated with empathy, perspective-taking, and understanding social cues (Bukowski et al., 2018). This development is vital for the maturation of the prefrontal cortex's connections to the limbic system, further enhancing emotional regulation and cognitive control (Steinberg, 2014).

The right to play

At the time of writing this book, there are 196 countries that have ratified the United Nations Convention on the Rights of the Child (UNCRC) (United Nations, 1989). The United States is the only member of the United Nations who have signed the Convention but not ratified it. Within the UNCRC, there is a strong recognition of children and young people's inherent Right to Play, and Article 31 states that all young people have the right to rest, leisure, play, recreational activities, cultural life, and the arts (UNCRC, 1989). For most of us reading this book, our government has pledged to ensure this Right, and all other Rights in the UNCRC are upheld for all our children and young people, and these governments are held accountable as to how these have been achieved.

Not all of us know how to play. Play is an innate need within all of us but is also a very social experience. Play can be lacking from some young children's lives, and a child who feels (or is) on the outskirts of community will not gain experiences where they can learn to respond to social cues or know how to embrace their imagination. I have seen this first-hand in a previous leadership role with primary- and post-primary-age children. Initially, adult facilitation was required quite heavily with the young people we were working with. Initiating play led to some conflict or disengagement, and work had to be undertaken to role-model play so that they gained insight into how the environment could benefit them and show that they had freedom of choice, something some of the individuals struggled with due to past reliance of others guiding or making decisions for them in all aspects of life. Play is a natural part of being a human being, but if it has been lost, even for a short period, integrating it back into the routine can take time, and we will explore how we can do this as we move through the book. Do not be discouraged if the first facilitation does not go as you would have hoped. As it is embedded into the environment, participants will feel secure in feeling able to engage with the different activities. As you continue to cultivate its purpose, you are championing and promoting Article 31. That is certainly something to be proud of.

Theoretical perspectives on play and development

Jean Piaget's Theory of Cognitive Development suggests that play is essential for both children and adolescents to explore their environments and construct knowledge. Piaget argued that adolescents, who are in the formal operational stage of development, engage in play not only for enjoyment but also to experiment with abstract concepts and hypotheses (Piaget, 1950). During adolescence, students' capacity for hypothetical-deductive reasoning expands, enabling them to think critically and solve complex problems. Play serves as a platform where adolescents can engage in hypothetical scenarios and test their understanding of abstract ideas, such as through role-playing activities in history or science experiments that require problem-solving.

Lev Vygotsky's Social Constructivist Theory emphasises the importance of social interaction in learning. According to Vygotsky (1978), play is a critical context where adolescents engage in collaborative problem-solving, language development, and social negotiation. Play-based learning allows students to work together, share ideas, and co-construct knowledge, which enhance cognitive and social development. Both Vygotsky and Piaget's theories have been influential in shaping modern educational practices in Europe, where collaborative learning through play is increasingly integrated into the curriculum, especially in the Nordic countries, and although they are often considered as relevant to early education, their influence continues to shape systems as children develop into adolescents and to underpin the pedagogical approaches that we generally adopt.

Contemporary theorists have built on these foundational ideas to align with modern understandings of adolescent learning. Stuart Brown (2009) identifies play as essential for developing creativity and adaptability during adolescence, particularly as teenagers navigate complex educational and social environments. Brown argues that play is critical for mental flexibility and problem-solving, helping adolescents to approach learning with curiosity and resilience. His research suggests that adolescents who engage in playful activities are better equipped to manage stress and approach academic challenges with innovative thinking.

Howard-Jones (2016) integrates insights from neuroscience to suggest that play activates neural plasticity during adolescence. He concludes that creative and exploratory play stimulates brain regions associated with memory, attention, and executive function, allowing teenagers to process information more effectively. This aligns with educational strategies that incorporate gamification and experiential learning, which engage adolescents in ways that traditional methods may not. In my book on project-based learning (Cole, 2024), experiential learning was shown as key in students gaining autonomy in their learning and understanding the purpose of the learning environment. This might be a useful point to again reflect on your own memories of adolescence. Think of a lesson from your teenage years. What are the most influential ones that spring to mind? Was the teacher talking at you, or were you given space to explore and be creative? I would be willing to bet that it is the latter.

Jaak Panksepp's (2007) work on play and emotional regulation provides further insights into its role in teenage learning. He highlights how play stimulates the brain's reward systems, promoting intrinsic motivation and reinforcing positive learning behaviours. For adolescents, who are particularly sensitive to reward-driven behaviours, play offers a structured way to channel this sensitivity into productive learning experiences. As someone with two sports-driven adolescent offspring, I see how sports games motivate them in other areas of their school life, and I find it interesting how they set themselves academic challenges the same way that they often do on the sports pitch. Their experiences of play help them to navigate various other experiences that they meet.

The Self-Determination Theory (Deci & Ryan, 1985) further complements these perspectives by linking play to the psychological needs of autonomy, competence, and relatedness, which are particularly relevant during adolescence. Playful learning environments allow teenagers to exercise choice, develop skills, and connect with peers, creating a sense of ownership over their learning process and increasing engagement and motivation. All of us should feel secure enough to be in control of our experiences and be able to try out things, especially when we do not initially succeed.

Before we move through the chapters in this book, this chapter underpins the reasoning as to why play is so crucial in this important stage of life. We will explore some of this research and perspectives further as we progress and review why play is so vital not only for learning but for teenagers' holistic development and wellbeing. Reflect on what you have read in this chapter. What resonates? What do you view as a teenager? What does the Right to Play mean to you?

References

Blakemore, S.J. and Choudhury, S. (2006) 'Development of the adolescent brain: implications for executive function and social cognition', *Journal of Child Psychology and Psychiatry*, 47(3–4), pp. 296–312.

Blakemore, S.J. and Mills, K.L. (2014) 'Is adolescence a sensitive period for sociocultural processing?', *Annual Review of Psychology*, 65, pp. 187–207.

Brown, S. (2009) *Play: How It Shapes the Brain, Opens the Imagination, and Invigorates the Soul*. New York: Avery.

Bukowski, W.M., Laursen, B. and Rubin, K.H. (2018) *Handbook of Peer Interactions, Relationships, and Groups*. 2nd edn. New York: Guilford Press.

Burnett, S., Sebastian, C., Kadosh, K.C. and Blakemore, S.J. (2011) 'The social brain in adolescence: Evidence from functional magnetic resonance imaging and behavioural studies', *Neuroscience and Biobehavioral Reviews*, 35(8), pp. 1654–1664.

Casey, B.J., Jones, R.M. and Hare, T.A. (2008) 'The adolescent brain', *Annals of the New York Academy of Sciences*, 1124(1), pp. 111–126.

Cole, F. (2024) *An Educator's Guide to Project-Based Learning: Turning Theory into Practice*. London: Routledge (David Fulton Publishers).

Crone, E.A. and Dahl, R.E. (2012) 'Understanding adolescence as a period of social–affective engagement and goal flexibility', *Nature Reviews Neuroscience*, 13, pp. 636–650.

Deci, E.L. and Ryan, R.M. (1985) *Intrinsic Motivation and Self-Determination in Human Behavior*. New York: Plenum.

Diamond, A. and Ling, D.S. (2016) 'Conclusions about interventions, programmes and approaches for improving executive functions that appear justified and those that, despite much hype, do not', *Developmental Cognitive Neuroscience*, 18, pp. 34–48.

Elkind, D. (2007) *The Power of Play: Learning What Comes Naturally*. Cambridge, MA: Da Capo Press.

Galván, A. (2010) 'Adolescent development of the reward system', *Frontiers in Human Neuroscience*, 4, p. 6.

Goodreads (2025) Bernard Shaw quotes. Available at: https://www.goodreads.com/

Granic, I., Lobel, A. and Engels, R.C.M.E. (2014) 'The benefits of playing video games', *American Psychologist*, 69(1), pp. 66–78.

Howard-Jones, P. (2016) *Evolution of the Learning Brain: Or How You Got to Be So Smart*. Abingdon: Routledge.

Kane, M.J. (2016) *Play and Adolescent Development: A Cognitive Perspective*. London: Springer.

Kolb, B., Gibb, R. and Robinson, T.E. (2003) 'Brain plasticity and behaviour', *Current Directions in Psychological Science*, 12 (1), pp. 1–5.

Lester, S. and Russell, W. (2010) *Children's Right to Play: An Examination of the Importance of Play in the Lives of Children Worldwide*. The Hague: Bernard van Leer Foundation.

Luna, B., Marek, S., Larsen, B., Tervo-Clemmens, B. and Chahal, R. (2015) 'An integrative model of the maturation of cognitive control', *Annual Review of Neuroscience*, 38, pp. 151–170.

Panksepp, J. (2007) 'Neuroscience of the early social–emotional development: Insights from affective neuroscience', *Current Directions in Psychological Science*, 16(6), pp. 370–377.

Paus, T., Keshavan, M. and Giedd, J.N. (2008) 'Why do many psychiatric disorders emerge during adolescence?', *Nature Reviews Neuroscience*, 9(12), pp. 947–957.

Pellegrini, A.D. (2009) *The Role of Play in Human Development*. New York: Oxford University Press.

Pellegrini, A.D. and Smith, P.K. (1998) 'Physical activity play: The nature and function of a neglected aspect of play', *Child Development*, 69(3), pp. 577–598.

Piaget, J. (1950) *The Psychology of Intelligence*. London: Routledge and Kegan Paul.

Romeo, R.D. (2017) 'The impact of stress on the structure of the adolescent brain: implications for adolescent mental health', *Brain Research*, 1654, pp. 185–191.

Spencer, R.M.C., Sun, M., Logan, S.W. and Coxon, J.P. (2020) 'The role of physical activity and sleep in adolescent brain development', *Frontiers in Psychology*, 11, p. 604746.

Steinberg, L. (2014) *Age of Opportunity: Lessons from the New Science of Adolescence*. Boston, MA: Houghton Mifflin Harcourt.

Sutton-Smith, B. (2008) *The Ambiguity of Play*. Cambridge, MA: Harvard University Press.

UNCRC (1989) *United Nations Convention on the Rights of the Child*. Geneva: United Nations. Available at: https://www.unicef.org.uk/what-we-do/un-convention-child-rights/ (Accessed: 14 June 2025).

Vygotsky, L.S. (1978) *Mind in Society: The Development of Higher Psychological Processes*. Cambridge, MA: Harvard University Press.

Chapter 2

Gaining a sense of belonging and identity through play

Perfection does not happen in play; we make mistakes, change focus, and build trust with those around us. This can be a challenge to those past the childhood years as we live in a world, certainly in Western society, where we are constantly told we must achieve various goals, look a certain way, and conform in our behaviours. Play can stand in direct opposition to these pressures by allowing freedom, flexibility, and failure, without judgement.

Teenagers often articulate this pressure poignantly. During my research for this book, one 15-year-old shared, "You always have to look like you've got your life together, even if you're falling apart." Another added, "If you're different, people stare or talk. It's easier just to hide who you are." These sentiments echo a deeper struggle of being seen yet invisible, of being surrounded by people yet feeling isolated. One student said plainly, "School teaches us how to get grades, but not how to be ourselves."

Educators can challenge these assumptions by using playful mechanisms that invite creativity, spontaneity, and autonomy. For example, drama improvisation activities help students take on different roles and embrace failure as part of the learning journey. In discussions with a teacher in a secondary school, I learnt that they used theatre games to encourage students to act out versions of themselves in alternate futures, imagining who they could become, not who they had to be. Creative workshops where teenagers make zines or digital storytelling projects empower them to express their personal truths without the fear of right or wrong answers. Open-ended group games and project-based challenges can strengthen collaboration over competition and encourage appreciation of an individual's strengths. Through play, educators can create spaces where perfection is not required and authenticity is celebrated. Doing so allows teenagers to step away from the pressures of performance and step into spaces of possibility, exploring different situations and developing confidence in being themselves.

Vulnerability and identity formation

The teenage years bring with them a variety of changes that can leave us feeling vulnerable, and it takes time for us to find out what is important to us and

DOI: 10.4324/9781003562368-3

who we are. Vulnerability is such a strength in life, but during the adolescent years, the need to fit in can be much more overwhelming than in other stages of life. Adolescence is a period marked by significant physical, cognitive, and emotional changes, during which the need for social belonging and self-identity becomes crucial. The role of play in adolescence, often undervalued compared with its importance in childhood, can be pivotal in addressing these developmental needs. Through various forms of play, ranging from physical activities, educational activities, and social games, teenagers can explore their identities and form stronger social connections. Vulnerability is essential not just for developing a sense of belonging but for feeling confident in their future workplace. For future leaders and for the development of strong and positive relationships, we can educate teenagers to understand that vulnerability is not a weakness but a gateway to connection, empathy, and authenticity. Through this, they are more likely to become compassionate and effective communicators. Leadership that embraces vulnerability enables individuals to take responsibility, admit mistakes, and build trust. Brené Brown (2012) notes that vulnerability is the birthplace of innovation, creativity, and change, all attributes required for collaborative leadership in the working environment of the future.

Educators who work closely with adolescents often see the power of vulnerability firsthand. "When a student opens up about a struggle, it changes the whole dynamic," shared one secondary school teacher. "The classroom becomes a place of trust, not just instruction." Another teacher reflected, "I stopped trying to fix everything and started listening more. That's when the real learning began, when students knew I saw them as people, not just pupils." When we open up the learning and social environment for adolescents to express their emotions and navigate conflict as a social group, their emotional literacy develops and resilience is built in a positive way, so they know that their voice and opinion matter, whilst actively listening to those around them.

The teenage identity

Adolescence is a critical period for identity development, as noted by developmental psychologist Erik Erikson, who coined the term 'identity crisis' to describe the challenges faced by individuals during this stage (Erikson, 1968). Play, in its various forms, provides a crucial context for exploring and developing identity. Through play, adolescents can experiment with different roles, values, and social identities without the immediate consequences of adult responsibilities. For example, playing online games or engaging in creative pursuits allows adolescents to explore aspects of themselves that may not align with societal expectations, providing a sense of autonomy and self-expression (Turkle, 1995). In addition to exploring personal identities, play can help adolescents form group identities. Adolescents often use play as a means of establishing social groups, whether through shared interests in hobbies, sports, or gaming. Belonging to a group is important for adolescent self-esteem and emotional wellbeing, as it provides a sense of belonging and acceptance during a time when peer approval is highly valued (Steinberg & Morris, 2001). Teenagers are navigating a transitional phase in which they are trying to define who they are and where they fit in society. Play, whether it be role-playing in games or the adoption of various personas in social media contexts, provides a relatively risk-free space for experimenting with different identities and social roles (Erikson, 1968).

Social media: The pros and cons

With the rise of digital technology, social media has become a significant arena for play in adolescence. Platforms such as Instagram, TikTok, and Snapchat allow teenagers to engage in social and creative forms of play that are both performative and interactive. Social media offers a space for adolescents to experiment with different identities, explore new social roles, and gain social validation through likes, comments, and shares (Boyd, 2014). It also provides opportunities for creative expression, as teenagers can create and share content that reflects their personal interests, humour, or social concerns.

However, the playfulness of social media is often accompanied by challenges, such as the pressure to curate an idealised online persona or can heighten the risk of cyberbullying. These challenges put a spotlight on the complex and sometimes contradictory nature of play in the digital age, where the line between play and performance can become blurred (Marwick & Boyd, 2014). Nonetheless, social media remains a key site for adolescent play that we cannot ignore, offering both opportunities and risks for identity development and social interaction. I do not suggest that we *get down with the kids* and pretend to fully understand how these platforms are used and invade the private conversations that they interact with, but it is our duty to get to know the various apps and minimise risk where we can. Developing playful activities that allow adolescents to explore the risks, benefits, and connections on various platforms helps conversations to flow between educators and teens. Also, teens can use the skills they have learnt through these activities in the educational environment. I have seen students lose themselves in the creative process, designing social media posts and images for coursework, as an alternative to a conventional PowerPoint, and thoroughly enjoying themselves experimenting with colours and fonts to make something engaging for readers. It has led to students being more engaged with research independently, and they have been able to relate to it, showing the purpose of the task more explicitly. The task has also created the capacity to have conversations about how and what we share on social media, weaving in knowledge on how to keep themselves safe online.

Gender identity

Gender can play a significant role in shaping the forms of play that teenagers engage in and the meaning they derive from it. Research shows that boys and girls tend to engage in different types of play during adolescence, influenced by both biological and sociocultural factors (Pomerantz & Raby, 2017). Boys are often more involved in competitive and physical play, such as sports and video games, whereas girls may be more inclined towards relational and communicative play, such as talking with friends or engaging in creative, social activities. However, these patterns are not rigid, and gender norms around play are constantly evolving. For example, the rise of online gaming communities has created spaces where girls can participate in traditionally male-dominated forms of play, challenging stereotypes and expanding the scope of what is considered acceptable for female adolescents (Jansz et al., 2010). Similarly, boys may increasingly engage in creative or communicative forms of play, breaking away from traditional masculinity norms. These shifts highlight how play can be a site for negotiating and reshaping gender identities during adolescence.

Play offers teenagers a safe and flexible environment in which to explore gender identity and expression. Through play, young people can experiment with different aspects of their identity without the pressure of fixed social expectations. These playful experiences can ensure that the teenager has a sense of agency and can engage with authenticity, allowing teenagers to try out preferences, styles, or behaviours that align more closely with their felt sense of self. For gender-diverse youth in particular, inclusive play environments can serve as vital spaces of validation and belonging, where rigid gender binaries are softened and self-expression is encouraged rather than policed. As educators and youth workers, we can build spaces where there is empathetic engagement amongst peers, using play to develop a self-understanding.

Finding *flow*

Mihaly Csikszentmihalyi, a Hungarian-American psychologist, found *flow* to be a powerful tool to engage with learning and a theory that has shaped my own pedagogical practice when working with teens. Csikszentmihalyi's (1990) concept of *flow* is deemed a highly focused mental state in which individuals become fully immersed in an activity that is both appropriately challenging and intrinsically rewarding (Cole, 2024). During *flow* experiences, individuals often lose track of time, experience a deep sense of enjoyment, and report feeling connected to both the activity and the environment in which it occurs.

In educational settings, the principles of *flow* have been increasingly integrated into pedagogical models such as Project-Based Learning (PBL), which mirrors many characteristics of play. PBL engages students in sustained, inquiry-driven projects that are often collaborative, cross-disciplinary, and grounded in real-world contexts (Cole, 2024). When well designed, project-based approaches allow teenagers to work towards meaningful goals that reflect their interests, which increases motivation and the likelihood of entering a *flow* state. The playful elements of exploration, experimentation, and creativity inherent in PBL can reduce performance anxiety and support risk-taking, enabling students to learn through doing rather than passive absorption. In projects, I have observed students losing track of time and engaging in creative tasks that they may not have previously considered contributing to. They also find areas of the project that they can excel in, helping them to reflect on jobs they may want to do in the future. Encouraging *flow* in PBL also encourages joy in what we do. The way young people are approaching their working life is unlike in previous generations. They want to find work which is more balanced with personal life and that meets their intrinsic motivations. Being able to explore different aspects of working roles in a playful, teen environment can develop a keener focus and direction as to what they want for their futures.

Creating a playful and inclusive space for teenagers

It is our duty to consider how we make play, whether indoors or outdoors, accessible for all teens. Recent findings have shown that there are clear gender disparities in the use of parks in the United Kingdom; 34% of female teens utilise the space in comparison with 63% of male teens (Make Space for Girls, 2022). It is also noted in the report that 59% of females felt unwelcome in the park spaces as they were dominated by boys. This research highlights that we need to consider not only the layout and physical design of spaces but also how welcoming they are to all teens and ensure that inequalities of access are tackled through working directly with adolescents. Engaging teenagers in the co-design process of play spaces ensures that their voices are heard, their needs are met, and they feel they belong in the space. Outdoor spaces are even more inaccessible for those with physical disabilities. Reflect on the outdoor facilities in your local area. How many of them have paths, parking, equipment, and play resources that facilitate those with a disability to access? In my own area, it would take me thirty-seven minutes to drive to my closest inclusive play park, and I do not know of any that cater for those outside of the primary-age category.

Adults still approach teenage social time with a need to control and judge. Engage in a conversation with adults discussing teenage behaviour and activities they participate in outside of school, and there will always be some who want to box them away and tell them off for being a disturbance. We see this with the example of the Mosquito device, an anti-loitering system that emits a high-pitched ultrasonic sound that is an irritant to those under around twenty-five years of age. I totally appreciate that some do not want anyone, of any age, to loiter in spaces but what I do not see is us actively looking at where else they could go to spend time with each other. If we want teenagers to feel like they belong in the community, we need street lighting, benches, nature, and the arts visible. If we want our classrooms to be accessible, a place for teenagers to feel they belong and a valuable place to learn, we need free flow, movement, creativity, and space to think and converse.

References

Boyd, D. (2014) *It's Complicated: The Social Lives of Networked Teens.* New Haven, CT: Yale University Press.

Brown, B. (2012) *Daring Greatly: How the Courage to Be Vulnerable Transforms the Way We Live, Love, Parent, and Lead.* London: Penguin.

Cole, F. (2024) *An Educator's Guide to Project-Based Learning: Turning Theory into Practice.* London: Routledge (David Fulton Publishers).

Csikszentmihalyi, M. (1990) *Flow: The Psychology of Optimal Experience.* New York: Harper and Row.

Erikson, E.H. (1968) *Identity: Youth and Crisis.* New York: W.W. Norton & Company.

Jansz, J., Avis, C. and Vosmeer, M. (2010) 'Playing The Sims2: An exploration of gender differences in players' motivations and patterns of play', *New Media & Society*, 12(2), pp. 235–251.

Make Space for Girls (2022) *Parks and Prejudice: Why Girls Feel Unwelcome in Public Parks.* Available at: https://www.makespaceforgirls.co.uk/parks-report (Accessed: 14 June 2025).

Marwick, A.E. and Boyd, D. (2014) 'It's complicated: Teen privacy in the age of social media', in *The Participatory Cultures Handbook.* New York: Routledge, pp. 105–115.

Pomerantz, S. and Raby, R. (2017) *Smart Girls: Success, School, and the Myth of Post-Feminism.* Berkeley: University of California Press.

Steinberg, L. and Morris, A.S. (2001) 'Adolescent development', *Annual Review of Psychology*, 52, pp. 83–110.

Turkle, S. (1995) *Life on the Screen: Identity in the Age of the Internet.* New York: Simon & Schuster.

Chapter 3

Developing playful skills for future success

One of my treats to myself is regular trips to the nail technician. At the start of the appointment, I am asked if I have any ideas for colours. I do not know why this question always feels like real pressure, but I am sure many of you who frequent the nail salon will appreciate this feeling! We have a happy rhythm now. I say what colour I would like and then she works her magic, often having her own ideas of what I might like prior to my appointment. Watching her at work brings me such satisfaction. She plays with designs, colours, tools, techniques, and patterns. If she is not happy with how it looks, she wipes it off and starts over. Her aim is for the result to look perfect, but this process also reminds me of when I undertook my Playworker trainer and was told about a young child who paid diligent attention drawing a house, putting flowerpots around the windows, and taking consideration of the garden. Once the drawing was complete, the child strolled over and picked up a pot of dark paint, painted over the house and satisfyingly announced that it was nighttime. It triggered the adults' innate urge not to intervene and prevent nightfall consuming the drawing. As the nail technician starts, starts over, tries something new, I watch the process in wonder, enjoying seeing creativity close up. This professional is at the top of her profession, and her playful approach to learning keeps her ideas and techniques current and results in clients such as myself being told throughout the month how wonderful my nails are. We educate young people with this same outcome-based approach but frequently rush through the content to ensure that their brains are crammed with memorised topics to record when they sit their final exams. I, and most of you reading this book, will not be in a position to re-design how the educational system is set out (wouldn't it be lovely if we could!), but we are all in a position to challenge this system. We are all in the profession through a commitment to the young people in front of us, providing the students with the skills to prepare them for adult life. Rote memory is not the skill they require for adulthood. After reading this chapter, reflect today on what skills you are using and how much of the day is spent using the methods we use in the classroom. My expectation is that you will be incorporating creativity, communication, teamwork, and critical thinking – skills aligned to playfulness and not memorisation.

DOI: 10.4324/9781003562368-4

The theory of Ba

Ba is a concept that originates from Japan and was developed by philosopher Kitaro Nishida and later popularised by business theorists Ikujiro Nonaka and Hirotaka Takeuchi. The term "Ba" (場) can be translated as 'place' or 'space,' but it represents much more than a physical location. It refers to a shared context or environment where individuals interact, exchange knowledge, and co-create meaning. This theory can be utilised in the classroom or play space to support the development of the skills that young people require for future job prospects. There are four key elements to the theory of *Ba*, outlined below:

A dynamic space: *Ba* is seen as a dynamic environment where people come together, whether physically, virtually, or emotionally, to create and share knowledge. This space is seen as an enabling environment where all participants can learn, collaborate, and come up with innovative ideas together. Think of your learning space that is not one where we impart knowledge onto the adolescent but one where we can learn together, generating new ideas. As we continue to shift into a connected world through technology, this space can evolve outside of the traditional learning environment.

Types of Ba: Nonaka and his colleagues classified *Ba* into four types based on the kind of knowledge interaction that occurs:

- *Originating Ba* is seen as the physical or emotional space where individuals share their feelings, experiences, and mental models. This is where tacit knowledge is created and exchanged (e.g., face-to-face interactions). Traditionally, emotions were not aligned with how we approach educating. However, much research has been undertaken to evidence the significance of nurturing and listening to individuals so that they can thrive.
- *Dialoguing Ba* is a more structured environment where people discuss and externalise their tacit knowledge through dialogue, creating shared understanding (e.g., meetings and brainstorming sessions). How frequently do you have debates and discussions with the teenagers you work with? Teaching them these skills during adolescence can help them in their future careers. A playful approach to meetings can also generate more discussion and ensure that every individual's voice is heard.
- *Systemising Ba* provides a place where explicit knowledge is systematised and shared formally (e.g., databases, documents, and reports). We might not consider reports and databases to be areas that relate to play. However, the design and creativity that can go into the layout and consideration of what to include are playful thinking processes.
- *Exercising Ba* is the context where individuals learn by doing, experimenting, and applying knowledge (e.g., on-the-job training or fieldwork). This exercise is a learning process that allows for mistakes, conversations, and learning. Having the ability to explore and apply knowledge helps to focus the mind and play with ideas.

Interaction between tacit and explicit knowledge: *Ba* facilitates the exchange of tacit (unspoken, personal) knowledge and explicit (formal, codified) knowledge. According to the SECI model (socialisation, externalisation, combination, internalisation), *Ba* is crucial for the different stages of knowledge creation (Cole, 2024). The theory of *Ba* is one where social experiences, emotions, and playfulness are encouraged to stimulate growth and confidence.

A living, evolving space: The concept emphasises that *Ba* is not static but continuously evolving with the people who occupy it. It is shaped by the relationships, interactions, and shared experiences of those involved. How frequently do we re-shape and re-purpose the environment where young people learn and engage with social experiences? Typically, in educational systems, we might spend some time each semester or each year reviewing the content of the courses we deliver, maintaining a static approach to the curriculum for a number of years. We might make some minimal changes following feedback from students but still maintain an instructional layout design to the spaces we use. I challenge you to reflect critically on the spaces where adolescents learn and reflect on how the space can evolve to improve the interactions of those within it.

Why consider *Ba* when working with adolescents?

This theoretical model has been seen to cultivate knowledge creation and enhance organisations' ability to problem-solve, adapt, and come up with new and innovative ideas. *Ba* draws on playful mechanisms to boost the team's creativity and collaboration and encourages environments where people can *spontaneously* interact, share ideas, and co-create knowledge. Incorporating Ba into working practice encourages people to test new approaches while recognising that some of these may fail or not work for the organisation. If we incorporate this approach in the teenage years, we are preparing young people with the skills required for the future workforce. Through trial and error and experimentation, trust is established amongst the team, and creative ideas can be crafted over time to benefit the wider vision (Nonaka & Takeuchi, 1995). In a traditional learning environment, the hierarchy between adult and teenager is evident; this does not help them to be future leaders who embed the values needed across the global economy.

The space that adopts *Ba* is one where creativity is encouraged and unconventional ideas can be shared, contributing to a playful working environment. Ba's principles support play in adult-led environments, balancing the playfulness with more conventional structures that we see within organisations. However, it is this playfulness that is seen to develop psychological safety within teams where colleagues can share ideas without judgement from others, where the team pulls together to adopt a collaborative approach. When working with the *Ba* philosophy, the energy and enjoyment of work tasks can increase and hierarchical barriers are broken down, due to the encouragement of everyone's ideas being heard and the reassurance that outside-the-box thinking is an expectation from all of the team, no matter the job title. A job for life is no longer an expectation and people are moving across career pathways much more frequently than we have seen in the past. Young people recognise that if we feel unhappy in our work, we should move to a new post – something we can learn from this generation. This is why businesses and organisations are frequently spending more time considering how they encourage employees to share ideas and work towards tasks differently than they have in the past. If we want a productive workforce, we need happy people. Playfulness is key.

Ba in-action

Companies are increasingly adopting creative processes to boost idea generation and to develop more cohesive working practices. Organisations such as Google, Toyota, and IDEO apply the principles of *Ba* and with excellent results.

Google has always been known for its innovative and creative approach. When teaching on leadership and management programmes, I have frequently used photos of their offices and case studies from employees to showcase how leadership can look without hierarchy and restriction. The company's innovative ecosystem encourages ideas to flow freely and is a prime example of how *Ba* can look in action. Google creates 'Originating' *Ba* through its famously open and flexible office spaces, designed to encourage spontaneous interactions among employees. Regular 'Dialoguing' *Ba* takes place through Google's '20% time' policy, which allows employees to work on side projects to promote creativity and innovation. Their digital platforms and tools serve as 'Systemising' *Ba*, where explicit knowledge is catalogued and shared across the organisation. This holistic approach helps Google continuously innovate, allowing it to stay at the forefront of the technology.

The organisation has gone through some challenges over recent years to keep up-to-date with technology's rapid progression and artificial intelligence impacting greatly on how their platform is used. Despite these threats to Google, their parent company 'Alphabet' has been seen to have hit and maintained the two-trillion-dollar mark at time of writing (Hollister, 2024). Toyota has long been known for utilising an innovative production system, exploring new ideas to stay ahead and remain successful. The company's focus on developing spaces where employees can interact at all levels to improve processes is one that can see 'originating' *Ba* taking place on the production floor, with workers sharing the tacit knowledge that is gained from the hands-on experience. Through meetings and regular dialogue, this help Toyota maintain its competitive edge.

Similarly, IDEO, a global design company, is known for its human-centred design approach and emphasis on collaboration to create innovative solutions.

IDEO cultivates 'Originating' *Ba* through collaborative teams that mix people from diverse backgrounds, encouraging the exchange of tacit knowledge through creative brainstorming sessions. They also utilise 'Exercising' *Ba* in the form of prototyping and testing environments, where teams work hands-on to apply and refine ideas. Through the utilisation of 'Dialoguing' *Ba*, open and constructive discussions take place across teams to support the development of the team and wider organisation. This interactive, fluid approach to managing knowledge in teams has allowed IDEO to consistently produce innovative products and services, with a culture that supports on-going knowledge exchange and creativity. With over 40 years as an organisation, this approach has helped IDEO remain at the forefront of global design.

What we see in all of these examples are company's working with vision and creating spaces that facilitate a playful mindset and autonomy over working practices. The dynamic and adaptive approach to *Ba* philosophy means that individuals can shift roles and duties and explore their own passions. This investment in people and playfulness increases idea generation and sees employees investing more in the organisation and wanting to stay with the company longer than they may in more conventional working environments.

Shifting from standardisation

In the United Kingdom, where educational policy has historically been more focused on standardised testing, there has been a recent shift towards incorporating play into secondary education, particularly within subjects such as drama, the arts, and design thinking in STEM (science, technology, engineering, and mathematics) subjects. Craft (2005) emphasises the importance of creativity in education and suggests that play provides a low-stakes environment for adolescents to experiment with new ideas, which is essential for developing innovation skills.

I work in Further and Higher Education and spend a lot of my time reviewing standardised approaches that also incorporate an authentic learning journey. However, we have not done enough across all areas of education to ensure that this authenticity is incorporated fully. There is no blame in this; the educational system lends itself to working along the same routes, following the same texts and imparting the same learning objectives. Learning is frequently not something seen as a joy by young people and this can limit them in their future career. In a report from the National Literacy Trust (2024), it was noted that only one in five children between 8 and 18 years of age read for pleasure and one in nine write in their free time. Reflect on your own experiences of reading and writing for enjoyment; I am sure I am not alone that these periods provide me with an opportunity to clear my mind, use my imagination, and generate new ideas for me to use in different areas of my life. Providing space within adolescents' learning environment where they can play with texts and explore ideas ensures that young people can establish the strategies to see the purpose of education and build on their skills for learning. Instead of standardising the texts and assignments we embed, we should *plant the seed*, exploring ideas led by the young people through project work that allows them the pleasure of finding out information for themselves.

Corporate cultures of the future

Richard Branson, a household name, has had huge success in the world of business. With over 400 businesses world-wide, his innovative and creative approach has supported his continual growth and he is recognised as a role model to many. On many occasions, Branson has shared that his educational experience was not an easy one: sitting at the back of the class, often not being sure what was happening, and receiving negative reports from his teachers, who labelled him as 'lazy and stupid' (Davis, 2017).

Branson's approach embraces lifelong learning, and he sees life as the ultimate school. This reflects in the corporate culture that he has developed, which is anything but conventional. At Virgin, he has cultivated a workplace that thrives on fun, creativity, and risk-taking, believing that work should be an enjoyable adventure rather than a rigid obligation. His leadership style sets the tone for this philosophy, creating an environment where employees feel encouraged to experiment, push boundaries, and embrace playfulness in their daily work.

One of the most visible aspects of Virgin's culture is the emphasis on fun. Employees are encouraged to engage in themed office days, social events, and creative challenges designed to keep the workplace lively and engaging. Branson himself leads by example, participating in high-profile stunts that showcase his playful leadership. From dressing as a flight attendant after losing a bet to driving a tank through Times Square to promote Virgin Cola, he sends a clear message with his antics: business does not have to be boring. These moments not only entertain but also reinforce Virgin's brand identity as bold, rebellious, and innovative.

Beyond fun and games, Virgin's culture is deeply rooted in risk-taking and experimentation. Branson's famous motto, 'Screw it, let's do it!', reflects the company's willingness to challenge norms and explore unconventional ideas. Employees are given the freedom to take creative risks without the fear of failure, knowing that innovation often comes from pushing boundaries. This mindset has allowed Virgin to expand into diverse industries, from music and airlines to space travel, always with a spirit of daring exploration.

Branson also prioritises employee wellbeing, ensuring that Virgin remains a place where people enjoy coming to work. The company was one of the first to introduce unlimited holiday days, trusting employees to manage their own time effectively. Many Virgin offices include game rooms, relaxation areas, and social spaces, reinforcing the belief that a playful environment leads to greater productivity and collaboration. By encouraging fun and promoting flexibility, Virgin has created a culture where employees feel valued and motivated.

This playful approach extends beyond internal operations into Virgin's branding and marketing. Campaigns often use humour and unconventional messaging, such as the cheeky *Don't Fly Virgin* reverse psychology ad, which challenged traditional corporate advertising norms. This willingness to break the rules and inject personality into the brand has helped Virgin stand out in competitive industries. Branson's playful corporate culture has had a profound impact on his company's success. Employees are engaged, creative problem-solving is encouraged, and the company has built a strong, distinctive identity. By making work an adventure, Branson has proven that a business can be both highly successful and incredibly fun. If we want to place value on financial wealth, he is also a billionaire and one of the UK's richest entrepreneurs. I obviously cannot comment personally, but he also presents huge success in other areas of life, with strong relationships with his family and his connection to the natural world, spending most of his time on the private, self-sustaining, Necker Island. I hope his past teachers had a word with themselves about the comments made about his ability to succeed.

From all the business case studies that we have reviewed in this chapter, we see how important playfulness is not only for financial growth but also for creating a dynamic and successful team. The Western education system was set up for a world where people were streamlined into particular roles in the future (consider blue- and white-collar pathways). This is not something that the world needs. Automation and robotics are replacing the role of factory workers, artificial intelligence is managing production lines, and it is reported that by 2030 robots will replace up to 20 million factory workers jobs (BBC, 2019). To develop and prepare adolescents to be competent for the evolving workforce, we need to encourage the creative thinkers, the visionaries, and the team players.

References

BBC (2019) 'Robots to replace 20 million factory jobs by 2030', *BBC News*, 26 June. Available at: https://www.bbc.com/news/technology-48760799 (Accessed: 14 June 2025).

Cole, F. (2024) *An Educator's Guide to Project-Based Learning: Turning Theory into Practice*. London: Routledge (David Fulton Publishers).

Craft, A. (2005) *Creativity in Schools: Tensions and Dilemmas*. Abingdon: Routledge.

Davis, E. (2017) 'Entrepreneur Stories: How Richard Branson's Dyslexia Trained Him for Success', *4over4.com*, 28 July. Available at: https://www.4over4.com/content-hub/stories/entrepreneur-stories-how-richard-bransons-dyslexia-trained-him-for-success (Accessed: 14 June 2025).

Hollister, S. (2024) 'Google is officially a $2 trillion company', *The Verge*, 26 April. Available at: https://www.theverge.com/24140489/google-alphabet-q1-2024-earnings-revenue (Accessed: 14 June 2025).

National Literacy Trust (2024) *Children and Young People's Reading Engagement in 2024: Annual Literacy Survey Report*. London: National Literacy Trust. Available at: https://literacytrust.org.uk (Accessed: 14 June 2025).

Nonaka, I. and Takeuchi, H. (1995) *The Knowledge-Creating Company: How Japanese Companies Create the Dynamics of Innovation*. Oxford: Oxford University Press.

Chapter 4

The benefits of play for emotional health and wellbeing

As a leader in an educational setting, I was on the perimeter during the induction programme of new students at the start of the academic year and was more in a 'backstage' position to support a variety of teams in the new term. This led to me coming into the classroom during the second week, when the main lessons were now timetabled, and we were ready to focus on the units we would be working on over the next semester. That morning, I reviewed my scheme of work, considered how I could engage students with the project-based approach adopted, and considered how to bring a heavy unit to life that requires the learner to undertake research and reading to develop their coursework. I updated hand-outs and reading lists, reviewed the brief, and then walked into the classroom, and it all felt wrong. We did not know each other yet. For the students to trust me with their ideas, creativity, and reflections over the coming term, we first needed to play. This meant not a series of icebreakers that left everyone feeling awkward but instead an opportunity to connect side-by-side and begin to gain a sense of the expectations I have of the classroom environment. It provided time to show the value of play and begin to hear from them what their expectations were too.

I began by explaining why play is an important value to me and how play can provide us with autonomy to create, test, experiment, reflect, and evaluate. The lesson started with students being provided with a page with the curve below and some pens. It was up to them to use their imagination and share a vision.

It may seem like a simple task, but as we created, we discussed how we use creative avenues to find flow and relaxation. I asked if the students had used mind-mapping in the past and showed them my own mechanisms for planning writing projects/presentations, and at the end of the activity, we were able to see the many ways the students had used the curve. This opened up dialogue for us to explore the value of difference and the importance of seeing things from another's perspective. Another discussion we were able to have was an honest reflection as to how we felt approaching the activity. Some of us felt a little anxious about starting. Some worried about their artistic capabilities. Five minutes in, all told me they were enjoying the process and liked the time

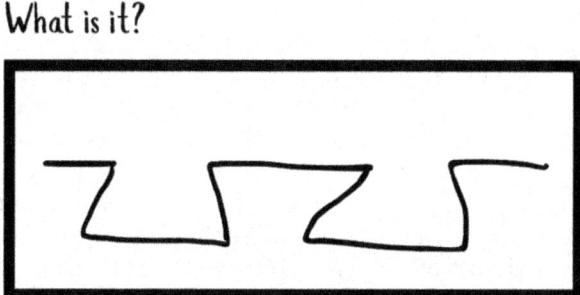

Figure 4.1 Image taken by the author Fey Cole.

Figure 4.2 Image taken by the author Fey Cole.

to do something with limited restrictions. I could sense play being the crucial connection to bond us and build the trust required for the classroom.

Traditional curriculum design can leave us restricted to following a tight schedule, incorporating teaching methods that provide students with the ability to memorise rather than to learn and investigate. It can also prevent us from developing bonds with the people we spend large periods of the day with. That does not lend itself to developing relationships and feeling secure in our surroundings. As educators, we are tasked with an exceptional workload to get through in the academic year, and it can feel challenging to try to embed anything else in. However, building the foundations brings better outcomes later. As we see more and more young people disengaged from education, we must reflect on how we approach things differently so that they can feel confident in the tasks in front of them. In the academic year of 2022/23, nearly 200,000 pupils, a third of adolescents in mainstream education, did not gain a grade four or above in English and Maths (Education DataLab, 2024). To study these subjects from our Early Years and not achieve a qualification at the end of it evidences that something must change.

Building adolescents' emotional competencies

Confidence is a crucial factor in adolescent development, significantly influencing students' academic performance and social interactions. According to Ryan and Deci (2000), the Self-Determination Theory is critical to focus on, and confidence is one of the three basic psychological needs that build intrinsic motivation and psychological wellbeing. If integrating the Self-Determination Theory into our approach, we need to recognise three key areas:

Autonomy: Adolescents need to feel that they have choice and freedom over their behaviours.
Competence: Adolescents need to understand the skills required to undertake a task. This allows them to recognise how to achieve their goals.
Relatedness: To thrive, adolescents need to form positive relationships, where they feel their voices matter and people take the time to understand them.

The above does not lend itself to the traditional classroom. A playful learning environment does. Education is not just about the learning objectives within the curriculum but also about the wider skills that support us to feel we can set our goals high and look to the future. If we have been in a classroom learning a subject for over a decade of our life and still do not understand it, this prevents us from looking to the future. Our barriers go up and we lose the spark needed to engage. Take some time now to consider an area that you teach where the young people have been struggling to connect with the content. How could you adopt a playful approach to focus on the three areas of the Self-Determination Theory? Plan below and make sure to reflect on what the outcome of this approach brought both for the students and for you.

Learning objective:	Embedding autonomy:	Developing competence skills:	Fostering relatedness:	Underpinning playful principles:

This approach will not change things overnight. It requires dedication and perseverance, but it will frequently engage those who have not been interacting, supporting individuals to feel more confident in participating and at ease with themselves as this approach provides permission to make mistakes without judgement. This not only supports academic achievement but also builds capacity to feel good in one's own ability, essential for emotional wellbeing.

Embedding play into the academic routine

Playful pedagogy, with its focus on exploration and creativity, has the potential to reduce academic anxiety by providing a more supportive and flexible learning environment. According to Fredrickson's (2001) broaden-and-build theory of positive emotions, positive experiences such as play can broaden individuals' attention and cognitive resources, allowing them to approach academic challenges with greater creativity and resilience. By creating a more enjoyable learning experience, playful pedagogical methods can increase students' intrinsic motivation. Students who are engaged in playful learning activities are more likely to pursue knowledge for the sake of curiosity and enjoyment rather than merely to achieve external rewards such as grades (Deci & Ryan, 2000). This shift from extrinsic to intrinsic motivation can lead to more sustained engagement with learning materials, improved academic performance, and a more positive attitude towards school.

The inclusion of play in the curriculum can serve as an effective means of reducing stress and fostering emotional regulation amongst teenagers. Pellegrini and Smith (1998) found that physical play during school breaktimes helps adolescents manage stress, which can lead to improved concentration and performance in academic tasks. In countries such as Japan and South Korea, where students face immense pressure to perform well in high-stakes exams, extracurricular play activities offer a break from the academic pressures, allowing students to relax and recharge. Sports provide a healthy way for students to channel their frustrations and anxieties into physical activity whilst releasing endorphins and helping to regulate mood.

Growth mindset

Dweck's (2006) mindset theory highlights the role of play in promoting a Growth Mindset, where students learn to view challenges as opportunities for growth rather than threats to their self-esteem. Playful activities that encourage experimentation without fear of failure, such as collaborative projects or artistic expression, help students to develop resilience and emotional intelligence. By integrating play, educators can cultivate an environment where failure is seen as part of the learning process rather than a definitive measure of a student's abilities.

Play has been shown to reduce stress and promote emotional wellbeing in adolescents, which is particularly important given the increasing mental health challenges faced by teenagers in Europe. In Finland, where student wellbeing is a central focus of the education system, schools incorporate regular breaks for unstructured play throughout the school day, allowing students to manage stress and avoid burnout. Lahtero and Risku (2014) found that students who had more opportunities for play during the school day reported lower levels of anxiety and improved emotional resilience. With one in five children and young people in England and Wales reported as having a mental health problem (Mind, 2024), it is critical that we review the impact their time at school has on adolescents' emotional health. Of course, there are other areas of children and young people's lives that are relevant to their emotional wellbeing, but if we spend about 10,000 hours of our lives in formal education, and this equates to around 20% of the adolescents' routine, we need to ensure that this is a happy and healthy environment for them to be in.

Scheduling free time

In Germany, the concept of *Freizeit* (free time) is integrated into the school day, providing students with opportunities for both physical and creative play. Research by Grünke and Cavendish (2016) found that students who engaged in regular physical play, such as sports or outdoor games, exhibited better emotional regulation and lower levels of school-related stress. This is especially important within countries such as those within the United Kingdom, where academic pressures and exam stress are significant concerns for teenagers. On the National Health Service guidelines (Why we should sit less, 2024), we are told we should be sitting less and reminding ourselves to move every 30 minutes. In the midst of exam studies and working towards coursework, the adolescent will be working in a seated space for an extended period of time, spending downtime scrolling through their phone in the same confined position. This approach leads to the young person missing out on the recommended movement that is required for physical and mental health. By promoting breaks and spaces for play, we are role-modelling its vital importance for healthy minds and body.

Exploring the big topics

Emotionally, play during adolescence offers a space for self-exploration and stress relief. Teenage years often come with emotionally turbulent times, as adolescents grapple with identity formation, self-esteem, and social pressures. Play provides an outlet for these emotional challenges. Creative play, such as art, music, or drama, may allow teenagers to express emotions that they find difficult to articulate otherwise (Sutton-Smith, 2008). In addition, physical play and sports can offer emotional regulation through the release of endorphins, helping adolescents cope with stress or anxiety (Bailey, 2006).

During my research, a 15-year-old male told me how attending a boxing club had given him an outlet for expressing his emotions in a positive way.

It wasn't just the skills that he enjoyed developing but also the chats he had been able to have with peers in the environment. He discussed how being in this type of activity brought space to be more honest than he would be otherwise, and he related this to the playful nature of the club.

A 14-year-old female discussed how her love of singing provided her with a space to be creative, writing her own lyrics and exploring how her voice could be used to release some of the tension that had come from her routined day. As a mother of two keen sports adolescents, I see how the Saturday morning team get-togethers bring a sense of fellowship and release from the academic week. All of us need an outlet, and for adolescents, they need to find a space where they can express themselves safely, in an environment that encourages it through positive avenues. Play is a natural way to be able to do this.

Identity stereotypes

Once an individual reaches adolescence, they will have spent a large proportion of their life at school. Their place in a school community can often be viewed as set, and this can leave troubling times ahead for the *joker of the class* or *the troublemaker*. The labels aligned with individuals can stick from primary to secondary education and have a detrimental effect on the students' engagement with lessons. If we reflect on our own schooling, I am sure it springs to mind who this individual was; it might even have been you. The memory of this person usually brings with it a smile from their peers. It might even bring the same positive memory for their teacher. However, when individuals are stereotyped in this way, they are faced with a huge obstacle to achieve and use playfulness as armour to get through the school day. It is our responsibility as Educators to flip the narrative and consider how we can draw on this playfulness that they have been using as a defence mechanism to engage them with classroom activities. Very often, these individuals are ones that others look up to. Placing them in a leadership position can help to build their confidence, and creating an environment that provides the capacity for them to flip the playfulness they are using as a protection, as one that is encouraged as part of the learning process, can support a rewrite of the narrative and promote positive outcomes.

Adopting a trauma-informed approach to playful learning

As educators, we are aware that many adolescents will be coming to us with a lot of other pressures on their shoulders. Some of them might share this with us. With others, we may never be fully aware of their personal situations. What we do need to understand is that humans do not have the capacity to be curious when we are fighting through trauma. Trauma can leave us stuck in flight-or-fight mode, and when faced with traumatic experiences, we place very little value on our own voice. We need to understand this when adopting playful pedagogy. There will be a resistance to participation, and individuals will find themselves on the perimeter, even feeling more isolated than they might in the traditional classroom.

This is why embedding play activities into our classroom is so important from the outset. Not for the curriculum but for building and establishing a trusting relationship where adolescents can see that they are valued for their individual qualities and their contribution can be acknowledged and celebrated. Focusing on the foundations and creating an environment where they belong will support the teenager in letting the emotional guard down and can become a welcomed release from the stress they find themselves in outside of their educational community.

Mindful play activities

A friend of mine was running some online creative workshops. I thought this might be something my own daughter would enjoy, so the two of us booked in for the session. We were told to prepare an area with paper, paints, a tray, and some random bits and bobs from around the garden before we proceeded to spend an hour online with Isla, the facilitator, and others who had booked in for the workshop. It was a joyous hour and not one I would have naturally attended or have asked my teenage daughter to do with me, and I was very glad of the time gifted to me with my daughter through booking into the workshop. We explored how leaves and twigs responded to the paint, cut out words from magazines to make vision boards, and painted with anything other than a paint brush. As we sat on mute, the time spent interacting with creative resources provided us with a space to talk together. The activity was purposefully slow-paced to enjoy the process, and the two of us talked about what was happening in our lives. My daughter had been a bit unwell, and she had not been able to get out with her friends for a few days, and this provided her with some time to be social. She enjoyed the interactions with the other adults also in attendance for the workshop.

Stimulating the brain through play

In countries like Denmark and The Netherlands, schools place a strong emphasis on physical education and outdoor play as part of a holistic approach to learning. Research by Bailey et al. (2009) demonstrated that physical activity, particularly play-based physical education, enhances cognitive function by improving attention, memory, and executive function. This is supported by Ratey (2008), who argues that physical exercise stimulates the production of neurotrophins, which promote brain cell growth and improve mental clarity. With the rise in social media and phone usage, children and young people are spending much less time exploring social connections face-to-face. Haidt (2024) suggests that, from 2010, we have moved from a play-based childhood to a phone-based childhood and that this has contributed to a stark spike in mental health conditions and children feeling isolated in society. Consider when you last went out for a walk, threw a ball, or danced. How did your facial expressions react? How did you feel? I can almost guarantee that you found joy and renewed energy within this experience. You may have picked up your phone to take a snap, but I am sure that the screen was not the focus. If we want to see young people engaged, curious, and happy, play provides us with the capacity to observe these characteristics consistently, leading to healthier individuals both intellectually and emotionally.

References

Bailey, R. (2006) 'Physical education and sport in schools: A review of benefits and outcomes', *Journal of School Health*, 76(8), pp. 397–401.

Bailey, R., Hillman, C., Arent, S. and Petitpas, A. (2009) 'Physical activity: An underestimated investment in human capital?', *Journal of Physical Activity and Health*, 6(3), pp. 269–285.

Deci, E.L. and Ryan, R.M. (2000) 'The "what" and "why" of goal pursuits: human needs and the self-determination of behavior', *Psychological Inquiry*, 11(4), pp. 227–268.

Dweck, C. (2006) *Mindset: The New Psychology of Success*. New York: Random House.

Education DataLab (2024) *A Third of Pupils Miss Out on English and Maths GCSE Passes*. Available at: https://ffteducationdatalab.org.uk (Accessed: 14 June 2025).

Fredrickson, B.L. (2001) 'The role of positive emotions in positive psychology: The broaden-and-build theory of positive emotions', *American Psychologist*, 56(3), pp. 218–226.

Grünke, M. and Cavendish, W. (2016) 'Learning from Europe: what U.S. educators can glean from the school systems of Germany, the Netherlands, and Switzerland', *Journal of International Special Needs Education*, 19(2), pp. 59–71.

Haidt, J. (2024) *The Anxious Generation: How the Great Rewiring of Childhood Is Causing an Epidemic of Mental Illness*. London: Allen Lane.

Lahtero, T.J. and Risku, M. (2014) 'Research-based evaluation and development of leadership in Finnish basic education schools', *International Journal of Educational Management*, 28(7), pp. 696–710.

Mind (2024) *Children and Young People's Mental Health Statistics*. Available at: https://www.mind.org.uk (Accessed: 14 June 2025).

NHS (2024) *Why We Should Sit Less*. Available at: https://www.nhs.uk/live-well/exercise/why-sitting-too-much-is-bad-for-us/ (Accessed: 14 June 2025).

Pellegrini, A.D. and Smith, P.K. (1998) 'Physical activity play: The nature and function of a neglected aspect of play', *Child Development*, 69(3), pp. 577–598.

Ratey, J.J. (2008) *Spark: The Revolutionary New Science of Exercise and the Brain*. New York: Little, Brown.

Ryan, R.M. and Deci, E.L. (2000) 'Self-determination theory and the facilitation of intrinsic motivation, social development, and well-being', *American Psychologist*, 55(1), pp. 68–78.

Sutton-Smith, B. (2008) *The Ambiguity of Play*. Cambridge, MA: Harvard University Press.

Chapter 5
Challenging assumptions of play

By questioning narrow definitions of success and resisting one-size-fits-all approaches to education, the chapter invites educators to create spaces where creativity, joy, and critical thought can thrive. To truly prepare young people for life, we must not remove play—but recognise it as a lifelong tool for learning, community, and change.

In Western society, we do not always value play, and from a young age, play can be frowned upon as an educational process. As we transition from childhood to adolescence, there is an expectation that we will play less and focus more. Play can be seen as a waste of time, an unproductive process that does not lend itself to our more mature years. The synergies between work and play in the modern working environment are something of great value to recognise, and play is frequently utilised to encourage the staff team's creative thinking and positivity. Airbnb encourages their employees to share travel stories and experiences, hosting meetings in themed rooms based on popular listings so that the team can embrace locations from across the globe. The LinkedIn offices include game rooms, and the staff team frequently participate in trivia challenges. Google's playful offices have a policy of allocating 20% of working time for each staff member to work on passion project ideas. Meta facilitates hackathons for the team to play with new technology, and IDEO uses play as part of its human-centred design process. These companies are some of the largest across the globe and represent the future of the work environment. Yet we tell children to stop playing in their teenage years and to focus on revising the material within a textbook. We need to challenge the negative assumptions of play if we want our young people to thrive in their future careers.

Experiential learning

For John Dewey, play was not merely recreational but a critical avenue for experiential learning. In *Democracy and Education* (1916), he argued that play enables individuals to explore ideas, experiment with roles, and engage in problem-solving within a safe and dynamic context. Dewey felt that learning is most effective when rooted in experience, as it engages individuals in meaningful, active participation. He perceived play not as mere recreation but as a foundational process through which learners experiment, hypothesise, and explore ideas. For adolescents, play offers a mechanism to bridge the abstract and the concrete, enabling them to test their evolving cognitive and social understandings in a low-stakes environment.

Dewey viewed adolescence as a transitional period where curiosity and creativity could be developed through playful activities to cultivate deeper understanding and personal growth. He believed that education should integrate playful, student-centred methodologies to prepare adolescents for active participation in democratic society. Dewey challenged the assumption that play was merely a social interaction and showed play as a powerful pedagogical approach, in turn demonstrating that play is not antithetical to productivity but a means of cultivating intrinsic motivation, adaptability, and lifelong learning. His views were ahead of his time, and his work still provides great influence on educational systems around the globe. Embracing playful pedagogy was something he knew needed to be embedded into learning environments if we wanted students to see the value of learning and engage with materials.

Dewey's view of play is deeply tied to his broader belief in education as preparation for active democratic participation. He argued that schools should model the democratic ideals of collaboration, communication, and critical inquiry. If we consider how play might look in this context in the educational environment, group-based playful activities can be utilised to encourage adolescents to negotiate roles, resolve conflicts, and work towards shared goals, thereby mirroring the dynamics of participatory democracy. Dewey also championed the idea that play facilitates intrinsic motivation. Unlike traditional educational methods that often prioritise extrinsic rewards, playful learning allows students to engage in activities for the inherent joy and curiosity they evoke. This leaves us with a provocation for reflection. Do we as a society view educational organisations as a place where joy and curiosity are to be found and nurtured or as a place to obtain policy-driven statistics and outcome-based results? Educational environments should bring joy if we want individuals to fall in love with learning and see its purpose. If we nurture intrinsic engagement, Dewey concluded, we cultivate lifelong learners who are not only capable of adapting to change but also eager to contribute meaningfully to their communities.

Dewey and project-based learning

Dewey's advocacy for play can be seen in his approach to Project-Based Learning (PBL). Dewey's PBL framework integrates playful inquiry by encouraging students to tackle real-world problems in collaborative, exploratory ways. For adolescents, this approach bridges their immediate interests with broader educational goals, making learning both relevant and engaging. Dewey's advocacy for play challenges several traditional assumptions that have long relegated play to the domain of early childhood or dismissed it as an unproductive pastime. Historically, education systems have emphasised structure, discipline, and rote learning, viewing play as frivolous and antithetical to serious academic pursuits. Dewey's work challenges this notion by demonstrating that play is a vital mode of learning. In PBL, play is positioned as a dynamic process that promotes active engagement and deep learning (Cole, 2024). By engaging in playful activities, adolescents can explore abstract concepts in tangible ways, experiment with different solutions to problems, and develop a more profound understanding of the world around them. This hands-on, participatory approach stands in stark contrast to the traditional focus on memorisation and repetition. Dewey dismantles the binary that play is purely social and for leisure purposes, by showing that play can be both enjoyable and intellectually rigorous. This reconceptualisation of play as a productive and necessary component of learning directly challenges the traditional view that education should be a serious, formal activity devoid of joy and spontaneity.

Dewey's ideas also challenge the traditional hierarchical relationships between teachers and students. In conventional classrooms, educators are often positioned as authoritative figures who impart knowledge to passive learners. Dewey's emphasis on play disrupts this hierarchy by developing a more egalitarian and collaborative learning environment. Through play, students become active participants in their own learning processes, co-constructing knowledge alongside their peers and educators. This shift towards a more democratic model of education not only enhances student engagement but also creates an environment where students feel their voice is heard and understand that they have autonomy in relation to their learning journey.

Scaffolding learning

Like Vygotsky's Zone of Proximal Development (as discussed in Chapter 1), play can be utilised to stretch adolescents' abilities by encouraging collaboration and exploration within supportive environments. Vygotsky's ideas resonate with contemporary perspectives like those of Rogoff (2003), who views learning as a participatory process embedded in cultural contexts. Rogoff argues that play functions as a crucial medium through which adolescents engage with and internalise the practices and values of their communities. By participating in culturally relevant forms of play, adolescents not only acquire essential social and cognitive skills but also develop a sense of identity and belonging. For instance, Rogoff highlights the role of guided participation, where more experienced members of a community, such as peers, mentors, or educators, can scaffold learning experiences through collaborative play. This approach highlights how play serves as a bridge between individual agency and collective cultural practices, enabling adolescents to navigate complex social landscapes while contributing to communal knowledge and traditions. Her work emphasises that play is not merely an individual activity but a deeply relational and cultural process that shapes how adolescents interpret and influence their worlds. Mezirow's (1997) theory of transformative learning offers a complementary lens, suggesting that playful experiences can provoke critical reflection and paradigm shifts, enabling adolescents to reframe their understanding of themselves and their world. These theoretical perspectives collectively position play as an integrative force which bridges individual development and collective social transformation.

Schools and creativity

Sir Ken Robinson, an influential thinker in education, advocated for significant changes in how we approach learning, particularly emphasising creativity, curiosity, and play in education. His TED Talk 'Do Schools Kill Creativity' (2006) is currently the most popular TED Talk of all time, highlighting how many are engaging with this important debate on what education is. In his seminar, Robinson argued that creativity is as important as literacy, particularly in today's fast-paced and evolving world. Robinson claimed that traditional education systems focus too much on standardisation and testing, which limits students' creativity. He proposed that education should nurture creativity from a young age and that play is a key component in this process. For teenagers, this means creating an environment where they can experiment, take risks, and engage in learning activities that are geared not solely towards passing exams but towards developing the skills required for original thinking and innovation. Play, for Robinson, is not just about recreational activities but about a state of mind where curiosity and imagination drive learning. For adolescents, who are often subject to rigid educational systems, the concept of playful learning can be particularly transformative but can also be complicated for educators to implement due to the structure of curriculums and the political drivers of a results-driven approach to schooling. Robinson argued that teenagers, like younger children, learn better when they are engaged and motivated by curiosity rather than by fear of failure or the pressure to meet external standards. This approach challenges the foundations of our education system within the United Kingdom and across many countries around the world. Robinson's critique of our traditional school system, with rote learning, standardised testing, and a lack of creativity, can lead to teenagers becoming disengaged and losing the natural curiosity and love for learning that comes in playful childhoods. In Robinson's view, play allows teenagers to explore subjects in a more hands-on, engaging way. This kind of active learning is important because it can reignite their passion for learning.

The need for a paradigm shift

Robinson's work consistently called for a paradigm shift in education, one that values creativity and play alongside traditional academic subjects. He criticised the way in which many educational systems are rooted in an outdated industrial model that treats students like products moving along a conveyor belt. This system, he argued, categorises students based on narrow measures of intelligence, often marginalising those who do not fit the mould of traditional academic success. Play was seen by Robinson as a mechanism for personalising education and addressing the diverse needs of students. By incorporating play into secondary education, schools can create more inclusive environments where every student can find their unique strengths and interests. This approach would benefit not only individual students but also society at large by investing the resources into a generation of creative, critical thinkers who are equipped to address the complex challenges of the 21st century.

Feminist perspectives on play

Feminist researchers have significantly contributed to rethinking the role of play in education, particularly in challenging traditional, patriarchal notions of productivity and authority. bell hooks (1994) emphasised the importance of joy, curiosity, and play in creating transformative educational spaces. For hooks, play was not only a means of nurturing individual wellbeing but also a collective practice of resistance against oppressive systems. She viewed play as a subversive act that disrupted rigid hierarchies and created opportunities for students and educators to engage in co-creative, liberating practices of knowledge-building. hooks felt that playful learning environments develop critical thinking, emotional resilience, and mutual respect, particularly in marginalised communities where traditional education often reinforces systemic inequities.

For hooks, the value of play extended beyond the classroom to encompass broader societal implications. She highlighted how joy and playfulness can build solidarity and offer moments of respite and healing in oppressive contexts. In *Teaching to Transgress* (1994), hooks described how play enabled educators and students to reimagine education as a site of empowerment and transformation rather than mere compliance with societal norms. This perspective aligns with Dewey's belief in education as a democratic and experiential process but situates play explicitly as a tool for dismantling structural barriers.

Feminist perspectives also highlight the intersectionality of play, addressing how gender, race, and socioeconomic status influence adolescents' access to playful opportunities. Angela McRobbie (1991) explored how societal expectations around gender roles often limit girls' opportunities to engage in certain forms of play, particularly those involving risk-taking or leadership. Reimagining play as an inclusive and empowering practice involves creating spaces where all adolescents can explore their identities and challenge societal constraints. Our views around certain play for certain genders is still both consciously and subconsciously something that we see adopted within society (as explored in Chapter 8), limiting the access of different play activities dependent on what gender individuals are.

Sara Ahmed (2017) examined the emotional dimensions of play, arguing that joy and collective playfulness can build solidarity and resilience among marginalised groups. Ahmed's work recognises the importance of considering emotional wellbeing in educational practices and recognising play as a tool for building connections and resisting alienation. Angela McRobbie (1991) explored how societal expectations around gender roles often limit girls' opportunities to engage in certain forms of play, particularly those involving risk-taking or leadership. Reimagining play as an inclusive and empowering practice involves creating spaces where all adolescents can explore their identities and challenge societal constraints. Feminist perspectives can be utilised to enable us to explore assumptions on play and how it is generally accessed and valued within society. hooks, Ahmed, and McRobbie all saw the importance of play for building stronger communities and ensuring that groups are not marginalised within them. By incorporating play into classrooms, educators can disrupt hierarchical models of instruction and create environments where adolescents feel empowered to express themselves and co-construct knowledge.

Cognitive development and play

Chudacoff (2007) found that contemporary educational practices increasingly marginalised play, particularly during the adolescent years, despite evidence linking play to cognitive development. Throughout this book, we see the need to reframe play as an essential component of adolescent development rather than a mere leisure activity. This perception is rooted in societal norms that equate productivity with structured, outcome-driven activities.

The link between physical play and academic performance is supported by studies that demonstrate the positive impact of physical activity on brain function. The review by Singh et al. (2012) showed that physical activity enhances cognitive functions such as attention, processing speed, and memory, which are crucial for academic success. In Norway, schools that have extended breaktime periods for unstructured physical play observed improvements in students' academic performance, particularly in subjects that require sustained focus, such as mathematics and language.

Global integration of play into education

Dewey's influence on experiential learning has inspired several contemporary educational models across the globe, many of which integrate play as a key component in adolescent education. One notable example is Finland's national curriculum, which emphasises phenomenon-based learning (PhBL). PhBL is an interdisciplinary, student-centred approach that encourages learners to investigate real-world phenomena through exploration, inquiry, and problem-solving. Unlike traditional subject-based teaching, where knowledge is compartmentalised into distinct disciplines, PhBL focuses on broad themes or phenomena that cut across multiple subjects. In a PhBL framework, students might explore a theme such as climate change by integrating knowledge from science, geography, economics, and social sciences. They are encouraged to pose questions, conduct research, collaborate with peers, and present their findings in creative ways. Sahlberg (2015) observes that this approach breaks down the traditional barriers between subjects and promotes a more holistic understanding of the world. Research by Lonka et al. (2018) found that PhBL enhances student engagement and motivation, particularly when learners are given autonomy to direct their own learning pathways.

In Denmark, and now more widely across the globe, the use of LEGO Serious Play in classrooms exemplifies the benefits of hands-on, playful learning. Students use LEGO bricks to model and solve complex problems, promoting both creativity and logical reasoning. Nielsen et al. (2014) found that students who engaged in LEGO-based learning activities demonstrated better problem-solving abilities and increased engagement in learning, particularly in technical subjects like engineering and computer science. During a Curriculum Conference for other lecturers across the college where I work, I facilitated a workshop using LEGO Serious Play and found it a beneficial way to show peers how play could be used within the classroom to replace more traditional strategies for teaching. The experimental process design provides a space to think and explore and is used to promote dialogue and encourage reflection: a beneficial focus for educators continuing professional development. The LEGO Serious Play workshops recognises that leaders do not have all the answers and that success depends on hearing all the voices of the team.

While video games have often been viewed critically because of concerns about their impact on behaviour and mental health, recent research suggests that they can also offer cognitive and emotional benefits. In Chapter 12, we will delve into the connection between play and technology further, but video games often require skills such as strategic thinking, problem-solving, and quick decision-making, which can enhance cognitive functions such as attention, memory, and spatial reasoning (Bavelier et al., 2012). Additionally, multiplayer games foster collaboration and communication skills, as adolescents must work together to achieve shared goals. The cooperative and competitive aspects of video gaming reflect the more complex social dynamics of teenage play, helping adolescents navigate peer relationships in a safe and structured environment (Kaye et al., 2017).

Challenging assumptions of play in educational systems

Integrating play into educational models during the adolescent years does challenge traditional perceptions of schooling. By incorporating play, contemporary curriculum shifts the focus from passive absorption of knowledge to active participation and critical thinking. This shift fundamentally redefines what it means to learn and succeed within a school environment. One of the most significant ways that play challenges traditional schooling is by emphasising process over product. Traditional education often values outcomes such as grades and test scores as the primary indicators of success. However, play-based learning prioritises the learning process itself: the exploration, creativity, and problem-solving that occur along the way. Play is not just for children. It is the fundamental building block for understanding and knowledge growth.

References

Ahmed, S. (2017) *Living a Feminist Life*. Durham, NC: Duke University Press.

Bavelier, D., Green, C.S., Pouget, A. and Schrater, P. (2012) 'Brain plasticity through the life span: Learning to learn and action video games', *Annual Review of Neuroscience*, 35, pp. 391–416.

Chudacoff, H.P. (2007) *Children at Play: An American History*. New York: New York University Press.

Cole, F. (2024) *An Educator's Guide to Project-Based Learning: Turning Theory into Practice*. London: Routledge (David Fulton Publishers).

Dewey, J. (1916) *Democracy and Education: An Introduction to the Philosophy of Education*. New York: Macmillan.

Hooks, B. (1994) *Teaching to Transgress: Education as the Practice of Freedom*. New York: Routledge.

Kaye, L.K., Kowert, R. and Quinn, S. (2017) 'The role of social identity and online social capital on psychosocial outcomes in MMO players', *Computers in Human Behavior*, 74, pp. 215–223.

Lonka, K., Joram, E. and Bryson, M. (2018) 'Teacher education and student motivation to learn: The Finnish perspective', *Teaching and Teacher Education*, 74, pp. 253–263.

McRobbie, A. (1991) *Feminism and Youth Culture: From Jackie to Just Seventeen*. London: Macmillan.

Mezirow, J. (1997) 'Transformative learning: Theory to practice', *New Directions for Adult and Continuing Education*, 74, pp. 5–12.

Nielsen, L., Hansen, S. and Mabogunje, A. (2014) 'LEGO serious play: Building a participative curriculum for entrepreneurship and innovation education', *Proceedings of the European Conference on Innovation and Entrepreneurship*, pp. 718–726.

Robinson, K. (2006) *Do Schools Kill Creativity?* [TED Talk]. Available at: https://www.ted.com/talks/ken_robinson_do_schools_kill_creativity (Accessed: 14 June 2025).

Rogoff, B. (2003) *The Cultural Nature of Human Development*. Oxford: Oxford University Press.

Sahlberg, P. (2015) *Finnish Lessons 2.0: What Can the World Learn from Educational Change in Finland?* 2nd edn. New York: Teachers College Press.

Singh, A.S., Saliasi, E., van den Berg, V., Uijtdewilligen, L., de Groot, R.H.M., Jolles, J., Andersen, L.B. and Chinapaw, M.J.M. (2012) 'Effects of physical activity interventions on cognitive and academic performance in children and adolescents: A novel combination of a systematic review and recommendations from an expert panel', *British Journal of Sports Medicine*, 53(10), pp. 640–647.

Chapter 6

Taking a risk
Physically and mentally

Finland, often regarded as a global leader in education, places a strong emphasis on play-based learning, particularly in secondary education. Finnish schools integrate play into subjects such as science and mathematics through project-based learning (PBL) and open-ended problem-solving tasks. For example, students might design their own experiments in a biology class, developing creative and critical thinking, rather than simply following prescribed steps. As Kangas (2010) highlights, Finnish education promotes play not as a break from learning but as an integral part of the learning process that stimulates curiosity and innovation. Finnish schools prioritise student autonomy, trust, and low-stress environments, with minimal standardised testing and a strong emphasis on formative assessment and teacher professionalism (Sahlberg, 2011). This creates space for adolescents to take intellectual risks, explore ideas playfully, and develop resilience. Importantly, Finland's success is rooted in a willingness to take systemic risks, moving away from competitive models and embracing equity, creativity, and whole-person development. For educators elsewhere, this is a reminder that taking pedagogical risks, by incorporating more playful, student-led approaches, is necessary to ensure that all young people have the opportunity to flourish both emotionally and academically.

A culture of risk-taking

Sir Ken Robinson (2006) highlighted the importance of play in developing a culture of risk-taking, which he considered essential for creativity and innovation. In formal education settings, particularly at the secondary level, there is a strong emphasis on avoiding mistakes and achieving perfect scores. However, Robinson argued that this fear of failure suppresses the willingness to experiment, which is a core component of creative play. For teenagers, play creates a safe space where they can take risks without fear of academic punishment. Whether through drama, art, or other creative avenues, play encourages students to try new ideas, experiment with different approaches, and learn from their failures. Robinson argued that schools should cultivate environments where failure is seen as a valuable part of the learning process rather than something to be avoided.

Kapur's (2008) concept of productive failure shows that when students engage with complex problems without immediate success, they often develop a stronger conceptual grasp when later taught solutions explicitly. PBL offers an effective structure for embedding this kind of safe, playful risk-taking into secondary education. For example, a group of students designing a sustainable housing prototype might experience failed design iterations, disagreements, and resource constraints, yet through these challenges, they learn to adapt, reflect, and improve. This iterative process mirrors how designers and innovators work in the real world and reinforces the idea that failure is not the opposite of success but part of the journey towards it (Barron et al., 1998). As educators, we have the capacity to reframe failure so that the young people we work with do not label failure as a weakness but see it as a meaningful and necessary part of growth.

Responding to a changing world

The rapid advancement of artificial intelligence (AI) is challenging long-established educational practices, particularly those related to assessment. Traditional essay-based tasks, once a key indicator of critical thinking, are increasingly being generated by AI tools and then marked by AI-powered platforms, raising serious questions about the authenticity, creativity, and purpose of such assessments (Selwyn, 2023; Luckin, 2018). In this context, educators must reimagine assessment not as a process of evaluating static outputs but as a means of capturing meaningful learning through process, collaboration, and play. Purposeful, playful approaches such as PBL, performance tasks, and portfolio assessments offer richer insights into young people's thinking, motivation, and agency (Thomas & Brown, 2011; Resnick, 2017). These approaches enable students to engage in experimentation, iteration, and peer dialogue, moving beyond rote responses towards deeper engagement with real-world problems.

However, adopting such approaches requires professional bravery. Educators must be willing to move beyond traditional models, even in systems which reward conformity and high-stakes testing. This shift demands trust in learners, a willingness to embrace uncertainty, and the courage to redefine what success looks like in the classroom. In this period of transition, educational organisations must prioritise the development of creativity, collaboration, ethical reasoning, digital fluency, and adaptability – skills that cannot be effectively assessed through AI-predictable essays or multiple-choice exams (World Economic Forum, 2020; Craft, 2011). If educators fail to make this shift, they risk preparing young people for a world that no longer exists. Instead, by embedding playful, human-centred assessments that value creativity and resilience, educators can ensure that learners leave school with the confidence and competencies needed to navigate complex, uncertain futures.

Freedom from adults' intervention

My son and his friends had been talking about a camping trip for weeks. Every weekend, that was going to be the Saturday it would happen. Then he would arrive home after a satisfied day out with his mates and tell us it was going to happen next weekend. I sat and listened. My husband asked whether we should help them organise it and I said no, let them work this out themselves. So on the last May bank holiday weekend, the boys seemed to have organised themselves, and my son rang me and asked if they could stay out. I asked the usual Mum questions: "Who's doing it?"; "Are the other parents ok with this?"; "What will you do if anything goes wrong?"; "Is the site ok to camp on?"; and so on. He answered all my questions with ease. I had a think. Was I actually ok with my son staying out on his own? I had some hesitations, but I realised that part of my hesitations were concerns of what others would think. When that comes into my head, I know it needs banishing. I knew exactly where he was, could get to him in ten minutes (the other parents even quicker), and it sounded like a fun adventure. I said yes. He was delighted and asked if I could bring him a spare set of clothes, deodorant, and aftershave. At this point, I did intervene and suggested it might be an idea if I also brought a blanket. What followed was not only one night of camping but two, with night two requiring that I take him a packet of sausages and a frying pan. The life skills seemed to be kicking in! The camping trips have become a regular feature in the friends' weekends and holidays. The adults are redundant in their duties, and the friends have started to build their camping equipment between them so that they are not doubling up on resources and can have a bigger kit of swag by buying different items. They camp on the outskirts of the village and bring no disturbance to others. They take away what they bring and sleep when they get home: there is a lot to be said for a good bed at home over a grassy field for proper rest! When bumping into one of the other parents recently, we joked about the resourcefulness of the friends' capabilities and that we had no worries about them always finding their way home. The joke rang true: being provided with freedom, they were gaining skills and experience on making decisions for themselves. I am aware of the preciousness of life, but I saw the young teens developing decision-making expertise and looking out for one another. I could have gone with the gut response of what society tells me: they were too young to stay out on their own; teenagers out on the streets are problematic to communities; they were in danger from others as the young people were not behind closed doors; the list could go on. However, I leant into trust and believed that they had developed the capacity to be independent and ask for help if it was needed. I strongly believe that when the friends move into their later years, their camping trips will be looked back on with fondness. Too frequently as adults, we step in to make the decisions and to keep our children protected. Full disclosure here: I can be overwhelmingly protective of my children and ask you to ensure that any decisions you make on young people's experiences are ones that work for you, your organisation or family, the young people you work with, and their families. As an educator, I do not have (or want to have) the capacity to decide if the young people I work with will spend their weekends camping independently, but the reason I share this story is about the young people having autonomy and for us to properly analyse the reasons as to why we say no to certain experiences.

Positive competitiveness

Positive competitiveness, when framed appropriately, can be a powerful tool for supporting young people's emotional and social development. Rather than encouraging comparison or exclusion, healthy competition should emerge within safe, inclusive spaces where every individual feels they belong and has something meaningful to contribute. In such environments, success is defined not by academic attainment or athletic prowess but by recognising and championing diverse achievements whether that be in music, teamwork, innovation, or kindness. This inclusive approach strengthens self-worth and social connection, both of which are key to emotional wellbeing during adolescence (Ecclestone & Hayes, 2009; Deci & Ryan, 2000). For competition to be psychologically beneficial, it must be framed playfully and collaboratively, emphasising personal growth, enjoyment, and shared goals rather than ranking or reward alone. Initiatives like team-based challenges, cooperative games, or student-led exhibitions allow for playful competitiveness, where students are motivated to stretch themselves while celebrating others' strengths. Ensuring that opportunities are equitable, through varied entry points, inclusive recognition, and support systems, is essential for preventing marginalisation and ensuring that all young people feel empowered to participate (Flourish Agenda, 2021). By incorporating elements of creativity and autonomy into our pedagogical approach, we can provide adolescents with opportunities to develop their competence in a non-threatening environment.

Reimagining possibility: Dubai's vision for innovation and the playfulness behind progress

Last year, I had the opportunity to visit Dubai, and as I stood waiting for my luggage to arrive on the airport carousel, I read through the Eight Principles of Dubai (Al Jalila Foundation, 2019) that were displayed prominently, and I found myself intrigued by the work the country was doing. In recent decades, Dubai has transformed itself from a modest port city into one of the world's most technologically ambitious urban centres, explicitly seeking to lead in innovation, digital transformation, and the knowledge economy. This vision is not simply one of economic competitiveness but one of reinvention through imaginative thinking, calculated risk-taking, and creativity – traits that align closely with the playful dispositions often encouraged in progressive education. Dubai's early development strategy in the late 20th century focused heavily on physical infrastructure and global trade. However, since the early 2000s, and particularly following the UAE Vision 2021 and Dubai Plan 2021, the city has shifted its priorities towards human capital, innovation ecosystems, and digital transformation (Government of Dubai, 2016). The UAE Centennial 2071 strategy now places education, future skills, and innovation at the heart of its long-term planning, with a clear vision to become "the most prepared country for the future" (UAE Government, 2021). Dubai's strategic positioning reflects a deliberate pivot from reactive development to anticipatory design, using future-oriented thinking to shape the present. From visiting Dubai, reading about it in the news, and observing its global influence, I found that the country is a leader in the field for these particular areas of growth and innovation.

The role of playful visioning

What underpins Dubai's transformation is not just investment but a form of playful, imaginative leadership, a willingness to explore the 'what ifs', test boundaries, and create environments where experimentation is encouraged. This echoes Sutton-Smith's (1997) view that play is a form of adaptive variability, a way of engaging with uncertainty and generating new possibilities.

For example, Dubai's Museum of the Future, built to celebrate not the past but what is yet to come, is both symbolic and substance of this mindset. The Dubai Future Accelerators programme invites global entrepreneurs to work alongside the government to prototype new solutions, a striking example of playful co-construction between sectors. This culture of innovation also demonstrates what Thomas and Brown (2011) call a "new culture of learning", one where knowledge is cultivated through exploration, collaboration, and flexibility rather than transmission and control. Dubai's innovation strategy cultivates a learning ecosystem that mirrors how young people can learn through play by trying, failing, imagining, and adapting.

So what can we learn from Dubai's vision to inform how we approach teaching and learning?

We need to see play as a serious mode of learning. Just as Dubai treats experimental innovation as central to its progress, educators should recognise play as a key driver of curiosity, resilience, and future-readiness (Gray, 2013). Systems that marginalise play limit learners' capacity to think inventively.

Failure must be seen as a catalyst for growth. Dubai's innovation culture encourages pilot projects, sandboxes, and iterative development, the very conditions that young people need in schools in order to experiment without fear of failure (Resnick, 2017).

Educators need to look to the future. Just as Dubai anticipates future trends, educators must explore what learning could look like in a changing world. This involves not only digital literacy but cultivating creativity, empathy, and adaptability, qualities that emerge through open-ended, playful learning.

We need to see cross-disciplinary collaboration as key for success. Dubai's fusion of design, technology, government, and business exemplifies the power of transdisciplinary ecosystems. Education should move similarly beyond silos, integrating the arts, sciences, and digital learning in playful ways.

Transformation begins with imagination. Cities like Dubai are redesigning their futures through playful foresight. Education systems need to reclaim the power of play to equip learners for a world not yet known. To prepare young people for uncertain futures, we must be willing, like Dubai, to think beyond boundaries, embrace uncertainty, and treat play as a pathway to innovation.

The courage to change: What educational pioneers teach us about taking risks in education

Progress in education has always been driven by individuals willing to take risks, those who challenge dominant ideologies, resist social and political pressures, and place learners' needs and rights at the centre of their work. While education systems often emphasise compliance and conformity, the most transformative educators have been those who stepped outside of the status quo to imagine new possibilities. Their risk-taking behaviours have not only advanced education in their own contexts but also provided enduring lessons for today's educators, especially in a globalised and complex educational landscape. The lessons from these pioneers are particularly relevant to those of us working with play-based pedagogies, where we may also encounter institutional resistance or pressures to conform. Let's review those who have influenced where we have got to today and use their experiences to have courage to step outside our comfort zone and take a positive risk.

- **Confucius (c. 551–479 BCE)**: One of the first recorded educational thinkers, Confucius placed learning at the heart of moral and civic life. He proposed that education should be available to all, regardless of birth or status (Confucius, 1997), challenging rigid class hierarchies. He also valued learning as an active process, promoting dialogue, questioning, and reflection over passive memorisation. This is a vital lesson for today's educators: playful exploration and conversation can deepen understanding and human connection whilst promoting a dedication to lifelong learning. In advocating education for all, Confucius risked political backlash and exile, a pattern that echoes throughout the lives of many trailblazers.
- **Aristotle (384–322 BCE)**: Aristotle built on this legacy, viewing education as a means to achieving human flourishing (eudaimonia). He promoted a balanced education that developed critical thinking, ethical reasoning, and practical skills (Aristotle, 2009). Aristotle's promotion of empirical inquiry and critical thought challenged both traditional myths and dogmatic

thinking of his era (Barnes, 1995). Later, his works were suppressed by religious authorities during periods when rationalism was seen as a threat to theological orthodoxy. This suppression did not hinder his influence, as he is still frequently drawn on today.

Rabindranath Tagore (1861–1941): Tagore rejected British colonial education in India, arguing that it stifled creativity and imposed alien values (Sen, 2005). At Visva-Bharati University, he designed a curriculum infused with art, nature, music, and free exploration. Tagore teaches us that play is not an 'extra' but a vital means of learning: one that connects body, mind, and spirit. Tagore's work was politically risky. Opposing the British educational apparatus and advocating an indigenous vision of learning placed him at odds with both colonial administrators and Indian elites invested in Western models (Mukherjee, 2010). Tagore reminds us of the importance of designing culturally affirming education and the need to resist dominant external systems and ideologies.

John Dewey (1859–1952): Drawn on throughout this book, Dewey has been hugely influential on today's education, but his work was not without its challenges. Dewey believed that education should prepare individuals for democratic life, not merely equip them with facts. This was a radical proposition in the late 19th and early 20th centuries, when industrial-era schooling prioritised discipline and uniformity (Garrison, 1997). Dewey faced professional resistance, particularly from conservative educators who viewed his child-centred approaches as undermining authority and academic standards. Dewey's Laboratory School actively encouraged children to take the lead in their educational journey, through inquiry and curiosity, showing us that a commitment to this approach can successfully lead to rewarding outcomes.

Maria Montessori (1870–1952): Montessori's practice is still hugely influential in the Early Years curriculum and has been seen to influence curriculum models for older age groups due to the way in which it encourages free thinking and self-directed learning. Montessori faced strong opposition from church and state, yet her ideas spread globally, despite being banned during World War II when Germany was led by the Nazis. Her legacy reinforces the truth that trusting children's intrinsic motivation and creativity is not a naïve ideal but a sound pedagogical stance that may require educators to resist rigid institutional expectations. In a period of time when females were still seen as less worthy than men, Montessori became one of the first women to qualify as a Doctor in Italy and dedicated her life to speaking out on behalf of the voice of the child.

Lev Vygotsky (1896–1934): Vygotsky underpins a lot of the pedagogical approaches we adopt now in developing curriculums. When we ask children and young people to explore further, we scaffold their thinking to the next stage. This is a concept shared through Vygotsky's work, and he was a pioneer we have referred to throughout this book. Vygotsky evidenced that learning is deeply social and cultural and that play is a leading activity in child development (Vygotsky, 1978). In Stalinist Russia, Vygotsky's theories were also politically dangerous. His work was suppressed for decades in the USSR, and only posthumously did his ideas achieve global recognition, transforming educational theory (Kozulin, 1990). Yet today, his concepts of scaffolding and the Zone of Proximal Development inform global understanding of playful, collaborative learning. His story reminds us that advocating for play as serious learning may still meet scepticism but is worth pursuing.

Janusz Korczak (1878–1942): Polish-Jewish educator Janusz Korczak championed children's rights and democratic participation in education long before the United Nations Convention on the Rights of the Child. His orphanage practised self-governance and treated children as moral equals (Cohen, 1994). Korczak's ethical commitment cost him his life; he chose to accompany the children from his orphanage to the Nazi concentration camp in Treblinka rather than abandon them. In the Warsaw orphanage he set up, children engaged in self-governance and democratic play (Cohen, 1994), and Korczak believed that play is children's right and a crucial expression of their agency. For educators, he models how to respect children's voices and choices, even in the most extreme contexts where adult control dominates.

Paulo Freire (1921–1997): Freire framed education as a process of liberation and dialogue, not top-down instruction (Freire, 1970). His methods, rooted in participatory, playful problem-posing, empowered marginalised learners to reflect critically and act. Freire's risk-taking was political and pedagogical. His legacy invites us to design playful learning environments that encourage questioning, creativity, and social justice, not merely compliant behaviour. His pedagogical approach rejected the banking model of education, instead encouraging dialogue and consciousness-raising. His methods were seen as politically subversive across Latin America (Gadotti, 1994). Freire's work reminds us that education is a powerful tool for empowerment and justice and is often viewed as a political threat by authoritarian regimes.

bell hooks (1952–2021): I have drawn on hooks' work for a number of years, but it was only when writing this book that I found that bell hooks does not use capitals for her name, as she wanted to shift the attention away from her identity to the work that she did. hooks argued that education should be an engaged, liberatory practice rooted in intersectional awareness (hooks, 1994). She advocated for inclusive pedagogies that addressed race, gender, and class. hooks faced academic resistance for challenging traditional hierarchies in higher education and for promoting emotional wholeness in teaching (Ellsworth, 1989). She recognised that playful dialogue and embodied learning are powerful tools for healing and liberation, especially for those marginalised by traditional schooling. Her insistence on radical openness and joy in learning remains a challenge to hierarchical, test-driven education.

Sir Ken Robinson (1950–2020): I would encourage you to take a moment to watch Robinson's TED Talk, "Do Schools Kill Creativity" (2006), to conclude your reading of this section. It acts as a reminder of the importance of taking risks in education and why young people need a fresh approach to their learning experience. Robinson argued that creativity is as important as literacy in modern education (Robinson, 2006). He challenged systems that devalue play, imagination, and the arts, in contradiction to the Western approach to educational systems. His work reminds us that play nurtures the very capacities that education needs today: flexibility, curiosity, resilience, and innovation. Promoting playful learning requires challenging powerful discourses of standardisation and control.

Current educational trailblazers who have taken risks to bring positive change

We often draw on past influential pioneers, but a huge amount of work is on-going. Pasi Sahlberg, born in 1959 in Finland, critiques the Global Education Reform Movement (GERM), promoting a trust-based, equity-focused model (Sahlberg, 2011). Now working in Australia, he challenges high-stakes testing and competition-based policies. Sahlberg's work faces resistance from global education policy trends dominated by neoliberal ideology (Rizvi & Lingard, 2010). Indian educationalist Sugata Mitra demonstrated the power of self-organised learning through his Hole in the Wall experiments (Mitra, 2012). His work questions traditional assumptions about teacher roles and classroom structures. In 1999, educational researcher and computer scientist Sugata Mitra initiated a pioneering study that would challenge conventional understanding of how children learn. Known as the Hole in the Wall experiment, the project involved embedding a public computer into a wall of a Delhi slum, with no instructions, curriculum, or adult supervision (Mitra, 2012). The aim was to observe whether children without prior access to digital technologies could teach themselves basic computer skills and develop knowledge independently. Over the weeks that followed, groups of children, many of whom were not in formal schooling, gathered around the screen, experimenting, collaborating, and sharing what they discovered. Mitra observed that, without guidance, the children not only navigated the computer but also taught themselves to browse the internet, play games, and use search engines. This process of peer-supported, interest-led learning led Mitra to coin the term Minimally Invasive Education (MIE), a theory proposing that children, when placed in resource-rich environments, can learn autonomously and in groups (Mitra, 2003). The implications of the Hole in the Wall experiment were profound. Mitra argued that the presence of a teacher, while valuable, is not always necessary for learning to take place. In fact, he suggested that learning can occur spontaneously when children are given the freedom to play, explore, and inquire. This perspective challenged formal schooling systems that rely heavily on structured curricula, adult authority, and standardised assessments. There have been critiques to this approach, and researchers have argued that we must not devalue the role of the educator, but what this does remind us is that we must lobby for the right learning environment and investment into resources that allow young people to experiment and explore, alongside their peers.

Many pioneers are omitted from this chapter, and I would encourage you to continue to find influence from those doing the hard work, to bring positive change – yourself included! To conclude, I would like us to reflect on the advocacy work of Malala Yousafzai. Born in 1997, Malala Yousafzai risked her life advocating for girls' right to learn (Yousafzai & Lamb, 2013). Her activism reminds us that, in many parts of the world, access to playful, joyful education is still denied and that advocating for it can entail profound personal risk. Malala should be viewed as a role model who inspires educators to defend inclusive, creative education for all, especially for the most vulnerable.

What do you want to be remembered for? Use this chapter as a reminder that taking a risk can be hard but is so worth the investment.

References

Al Jalila Foundation (2019) *The Eight Principles of Dubai*. Dubai: Government of Dubai.
Aristotle (2009) *The Nicomachean Ethics*. Translated by D. Ross. Oxford: Oxford University Press.
Barnes, J. (1995) *Aristotle: A Very Short Introduction*. Oxford: Oxford University Press.
Barron, B.J.S., Schwartz, D.L., Vye, N.J., Moore, A., Petrosino, A., Zech, L. and Bransford, J.D. (1998) 'Doing with understanding: Lessons from research on problem- and project-based learning', *The Journal of the Learning Sciences*, 7(3–4), pp. 271–311.
Cohen, S. (1994) *Children and Play in the Holocaust: Games Among the Shadows*. New York: Holmes & Meier.
Confucius (1997) *The Analects*. Translated by D.C. Lau. London: Penguin Classics.
Craft, A. (2011) '*Creativity and Education Futures*', Trentham Books.
Deci, E.L. and Ryan, R.M. (2000) 'The "what" and "why" of goal pursuits: Human needs and the self-determination of behavior', *Psychological Inquiry*, 11(4), pp. 227–268.
Ecclestone, K. and Hayes, D. (2009) *The Dangerous Rise of Therapeutic Education*. London: Routledge.
Ellsworth, E. (1989) 'Why doesn't this feel empowering? Working through the repressive myths of critical pedagogy', *Harvard Educational Review*, 59(3), pp. 297–324.
Flourish Agenda (2021) *Radical Healing Framework*. Available at: https://www.flourishagenda.com (Accessed: 14 June 2025).
Freire, P. (1970) *Pedagogy of the Oppressed*. Translated by M.B. Ramos. New York: Herder and Herder.
Gadotti, M. (1994) *Reading Paulo Freire: His Life and Work*. Albany, NY: SUNY Press.
Garrison, J. (1997) *Dewey and Eros: Wisdom and Desire in the Art of Teaching*. New York: Teachers College Press.
Government of Dubai (2016) *Dubai Plan 2021*. Dubai: Executive Council of Dubai.

Gray, P. (2013) *Free to Learn: Why Unleashing the Instinct to Play Will Make Our Children Happier, More Self-Reliant, and Better Students for Life*. New York: Basic Books.

hooks, b. (1994) *Teaching to Transgress: Education as the Practice of Freedom*. New York: Routledge.

Kangas, M. (2010) 'The school of the future: Theoretical and pedagogical approaches for creative and playful learning environments', *Procedia - Social and Behavioral Sciences*, 2(2), pp. 2171–2180.

Kapur, M. (2008) 'Productive failure', *Cognition and Instruction*, 26(3), pp. 379–424.

Kozulin, A. (1990) *Vygotsky's Psychology: A Biography of Ideas*. Cambridge, MA: Harvard University Press.

Luckin, R. (2018) *Machine Learning and Human Intelligence: The Future of Education for the 21st Century*. London: UCL Institute of Education Press.

Mitra, S. (2003) 'Minimally invasive education: A progress report on the "hole-in-the-wall" experiments', *British Journal of Educational Technology*, 34(3), pp. 367–371.

Mitra, S. (2012) *Beyond the Hole in the Wall: Discover the Power of Self-Organized Learning*. New York: TED Books.

Mukherjee, M. (2010) *Rabindranath Tagore: The Modernizing Force of Tradition*. Kolkata: Rupa Publications.

Resnick, M. (2017) *Lifelong Kindergarten: Cultivating Creativity through Projects, Passion, Peers, and Play*. Cambridge, MA: MIT Press.

Rizvi, F. and Lingard, B. (2010) *Globalizing Education Policy*. London: Routledge.

Robinson, K. (2006) *Do Schools Kill Creativity?* [TED Talk]. Available at: https://www.ted.com/talks/ken_robinson_do_schools_kill_creativity (Accessed: 14 June 2025).

Sahlberg, P. (2011) *Finnish Lessons: What Can the World Learn from Educational Change in Finland?* New York: Teachers College Press.

Selwyn, N. (2023) 'AI and the future of education: Teaching in the age of automation', *British Journal of Educational Technology*, 54(1), pp. 5–19.

Sen, A. (2005) *The Argumentative Indian: Writings on Indian History, Culture and Identity*. London: Penguin.

Sutton-Smith, B. (1997) *The Ambiguity of Play*. Cambridge, MA: Harvard University Press.

Thomas, D. and Brown, J.S. (2011) *A New Culture of Learning: Cultivating the Imagination for a World of Constant Change*. Lexington, KY: CreateSpace.

UAE Government (2021) *UAE Centennial 2071 Strategy*. Available at: https://u.ae/en/about-the-uae/strategies-initiatives-and-awards/federal-governments-strategies-and-plans/uae-centennial-2071 (Accessed: 14 June 2025).

Vygotsky, L.S. (1978) *Mind in Society: The Development of Higher Psychological Processes*. Cambridge, MA: Harvard University Press.

World Economic Forum (2020) *The Future of Jobs Report 2020*. Available at: https://www3.weforum.org/docs/WEF_Future_of_Jobs_2020.pdf (Accessed: 8 August 2025).

Yousafzai, M. and Lamb, C. (2013) *I am Malala: The Girl Who Stood Up for Education and Was Shot by the Taliban*. London: Wiedenfeld & Nicolson.

Chapter 7

Never too old to play

Being a role model and advocate of play

In secondary education and colleges, play is often viewed as something separate from learning, confined to early childhood or physical education. However, research increasingly shows that play can serve as an essential component of learning for adolescents. But how do we, as educators, role-model its value and importance? Modelling a playful mindset and adopting a playful pedagogical approach can encourage young people to see play as a natural cycle within the learning environment and know that the space is safe to try out new things and put forward creative ideas.

Why is it important for practitioners to role-model play?

Play requires safety, time, and trust. When schools invest in professional development strategies that promote play, they are not just improving pedagogy but modelling a way of being that makes education more human, more connected, and more sustainable. The value of advocating for play is vast.

Enhanced social interaction: The teenage years can often bring some challenges with social dynamics but play creates opportunities for positive peer interaction. When educators role-model playful behaviour, they encourage a collaborative rather than competitive atmosphere (Gill, 2014). Play-based learning can lead to improved relationships between students and teachers, building a sense of community and trust in the classroom (Roffey, 2012).

Increased engagement and motivation: A classroom that integrates playful elements can be more engaging and motivating for students. Educators who actively participate in play show that learning can be dynamic and fun, making students more willing to participate and invest in their own learning (Sutton-Smith, 1997). This is particularly important for teenagers, who may become disengaged from traditional, lecture-based learning methods.

Development of critical thinking and creativity: Play often involves solving problems, whether through games or creative activities. Educators who

DOI: 10.4324/9781003562368-8

engage in these activities demonstrate critical thinking in action, encouraging students to develop their own problem-solving skills. This aligns with Vygotsky's (1978) concept of the Zone of Proximal Development, where students can achieve higher levels of understanding with guidance from a knowledgeable adult.

Support for emotional development: Teenagers face various emotional challenges, including stress, anxiety, and identity development. Play can serve as a form of emotional release, helping students manage their feelings in a non-threatening environment (Pellegrini, 2013). When educators participate in play, they model healthy emotional expression and coping mechanisms, demonstrating that it is acceptable to relax, laugh, and take breaks from serious tasks.

Experiential learning

Educators can be role models of play by embedding playful pedagogical approaches in their teaching. According to Kolb (2014), experiential learning that incorporates play allows students to connect with content in a more profound way, encouraging deeper learning. Through games, simulations, and problem-solving activities, educators can create environments where students feel safe to experiment and explore, which nurture curiosity and intrinsic motivation (Gee, 2013). Ways in which this can be embedded are through incorporating Project-Based Learning, which hands over autonomy of learning from educator to student. Incorporating strategies for educators and practitioners to practice experiential learning can be a great way to encourage the team to embed this into their own pedagogical approach. One way of doing this is through introducing an engaging challenge or simulation, in one of your professional development days, that reflects the day-to-day experiences of students, such as a group puzzle, role-play, or time-limited creative task. Whitton (2018) suggests that role-playing can deepen students' understanding by connecting theoretical knowledge to practical application, and it is the same principle when we are learning new strategies as educators. By building in structured reflection, you can ask participants to consider what they felt, what they learned, and how they might adapt the experience for their own students, introducing new activities that they can use in their classrooms or organisations. You can extend this by encouraging playful risk-taking by using materials or themes unrelated to formal content. I have used this as an exercise in one of our whole-college professional development days, introducing a task where attendees had to build an aeroplane out of Lego. As an advocate of play, I still felt daunted introducing this to so many people and worried about what the response would be. I should have trusted in play from the start as not only did everyone engage but there was a lot of fun and teamwork (and competitiveness!) that came from the session.

Playful mindsets

Beyond using play as a teaching tool, educators can model a playful mindset by demonstrating flexibility, curiosity, and openness to new experiences. Sutton-Smith (1997) suggests that play is not only an activity but also a way of thinking that embraces ambiguity and challenges. Teachers can model this mindset by showing enthusiasm for learning, asking open-ended questions, and valuing creativity and problem-solving over rote memorisation during their own sessions with young people. Resnick (2017) provides an example of this during maths lessons, with teachers presenting a problem with multiple solutions, encouraging the students to find creative ways to arrive at the correct answer rather than merely follow a set formula. A workshop can be delivered to staff teams by your play advocates to evaluate how play underpins your organisation's shared values. Linking values to behaviours can strengthen people's acknowledgement that play is an important strategy for learning. Creating a reflective session for peers, you may wish to ask the following guided questions:

What role does play currently have in our organisation's vision or values? Is it visible, celebrated, or hidden?
In what ways do our everyday classroom practices and staff behaviours model playfulness, curiosity, and emotional safety?
Are there contradictions between what we say we value (e.g., creativity and learner wellbeing) and what we prioritise (e.g., exam outcomes and compliance)?
How can we align our policies, pedagogy, and interactions more closely with a commitment to play as a meaningful educational approach?

It is important for the facilitator to actively listen to the responses that are given, and the session can be extended by asking participants to share their own experiences of playfulness with the young people they work with. This provides an opportunity not just for reflection but for the team to learn from one another.

The opportunity to fail successfully

Throughout this book, the value of learning through failures has been discussed. I recently listened to *The Diary of a CEO*, a book by Steven Bartlett (2023), who said in his talk that, to succeed, we need to double our failure rate. That comment stuck with me, as I reflected on going for a few job interviews before securing the position that I really wanted. I had not failed but instead put myself out there, something I could not have said prior to the interviews. The initial opportunities allowed me to reflect, decide what I really wanted, and find the role I really wanted.

Csikszentmihalyi (1990) emphasises the concept of *flow*, where learners are deeply engaged in an activity that is both challenging and enjoyable. By modelling resilience and a willingness to experiment, educators help students understand that mistakes are part of the learning process and that exploration and play can lead to innovation and growth, so it is important that teams also be encouraged to see mistakes as a learning opportunity. Educators play an important role in influencing the wider school culture, and by advocating for the value of play in learning, we can shift others' perspectives and increase playful pedagogical approaches within the setting. According to Bateson and Martin (2013), play has evolved as a means of preparing individuals for the complexities of life, making it an essential tool for adolescent development. Introducing sessions where practitioners can reflect on mistakes can be a powerful method for developing a growth mindset. A professional development strategy that can be facilitated to support this could be to invite staff to collaboratively explore how their setting responds to mistakes and whether those responses align with the values of curiosity, experimentation, and growth. To start, ask staff to anonymously write down a classroom mistake they've made that turned into a learning opportunity. Mix these up and read a few aloud to the group. This creates a safe space for discussion without requiring personal disclosure and without judgment, so set the boundaries in advance, so that individuals feel confident to share and explore the different situations. If this is a developing team that still requires trust to be nurtured, you may wish to use case studies instead. Once the stories have been reviewed, encourage discussion on how these moments could be reframed as opportunities, before inviting staff to co-create a *mistake wall* or digital space celebrating what went wrong and what was learned, modelled on the idea of playful reflection rather than embarrassment. This type of activity can build stronger trust amongst the team and support open conversations moving forward, embracing mistakes as learning opportunities. This strategy helps to dismantle perfectionism and fear of judgement that can block creativity, and when staff acknowledge mistakes as vital to discovery, they give students permission to do the same. Over time, this reframes failure not as a weakness but as a necessary part of meaningful, playful learning.

Outside of the classroom

Educators often overlook communal or transitional spaces as opportunities for modelling play. By implementing a strategy to 'reclaim the corridors' as a team, you can encourage staff to co-design playful interventions in corridors, lunch queues, or shared spaces. Allocate some time to make play visible across the setting, helping to challenge the notion that learning (and, by extension, play) happens only in formal lessons. Examples of areas you may wish to focus on might be co-creating a display with educators/students where weekly riddles or challenges could be added or using break-times for some staff/young people games together. Consider how to develop your outdoor recreational space to make it an extension to the classroom and be led by the creativity of those participating to develop a more playful environment. Remember to reflect on the areas that staff use as well: does your staffroom feel as playful as your classrooms? Do staff have access to activities that stimulate playful discussions? I am currently in the process of designing a workshop for a conference in England that is fully focused on playful approaches with those on Higher Education programmes. My workshop is focused on an outdoor session where educators and students can generate co-created ideas through a playful and creative doodle. I have used this in my own teaching approach and found that I get much more participation and discussion when using this strategy than I do when students are in a more traditionally laid-out classroom.

The power of music for playful learning

Following one summer day trip, my family put together a playlist of music that reminded us of one another. I have just had a look, and there are three hours and forty minutes worth of tunes added, and each one of the songs can be pinpointed to a memory of us all together. The daytrip that sparked this was a car ride up to the North Coast of Northern Ireland, and it was, for once on the island of Ireland, a beautifully warm day. As we sat in a bit of traffic as we headed back from the beach, a cheesy pop song came on, and my husband and I sang at the top of our lungs, windows open, doing some sort of sitting dance routine that bore no resemblance to what the pop band would have performed. We all laughed, the younger passengers told us to stop, we paid no attention and sang most of the hour-and-a-half car ride home. It was silly. It was fun. The children added the cheesy pop to the playlist. Music allows us to express our emotions and feelings in a way that cannot be done when sitting in a silent environment. In the setting, you can create a staff wellbeing book that invites practitioners to add to a working document, sharing highlights or moments from their week with the rest of the team. This might include a playlist of feel-good tracks, tips for maintaining good vibes during busy assessment periods, or a highlight of the week that brought positive energy. During the Covid-19 lockdown period, through the online JoyFE community (a community of practice that brought college educators from across the United Kingdom together), our friend Sinead Blackledge created a weekly soundtrack, and all of us submitted our favourite track that was linked to a particular theme. It was not only a playful moment to decide on the song choice, but when it came time for my Friday admin, the playlist brought me time to sing along and get up and move as I worked through my tasks. It also strengthened our community, providing a different way to share what we liked, be introduced to something new, and spark conversations.

The role of educators in modelling play

Despite all the benefits, play is sometimes de-emphasised in secondary schools because of the increasing focus on academic achievement and standardised testing (Jarvis et al., 2014). Educators play a crucial role in shaping the classroom environment and the attitudes students develop towards learning. When teachers model play, they signal that playful exploration and creativity are valuable within the academic setting and wider experiences. Modelling playful behaviour can range from participating in classroom games to using humour, creative problem-solving, and collaborative projects in lessons. These behaviours are then mirrored by students, who are more likely to participate in play if they see their teachers actively doing so. Importantly, this modelling helps normalise play as a valid and beneficial activity, reducing the stigma that it is childish or unproductive for older students.

Challenges of role-modelling play

Despite the clear benefits, some educators may be hesitant to model play due to concerns about classroom management or the perception that play undermines academic learning. However, research suggests that play can be structured in ways that support academic goals while developing creativity and engagement (Jarvis et al., 2014). Teachers may also worry about losing authority if they engage in play, but studies have shown that play can enhance respect between students and teachers when appropriately managed (Roffey, 2012). This is why it is so valuable to use strategies like the ones we have discussed to advocate for play and normalise it as a learning tool for *both* young people and staff teams. You may need to be brave and put yourself out of your comfort zone to lead and encourage these sessions, but the thing about play is that once one person engages, the invitation to laugh and engage alongside them becomes irresistible.

Reflection on play advocacy

As we conclude this chapter, take some time to reflect on the following questions and use them to engage in conversations with your colleagues:

What would it look like to treat your own playfulness as a professional asset?
What would happen if we made our staff rooms feel as playful as our best classrooms?
And how might our students grow if they saw us laugh, try, fail, and try again?

To be a role model for play, you must also be a participant and reclaim your permission to play. The United Nations Article 31 in the Rights of the Child states that every child under 18 must have the right to rest, leisure, and participation in cultural and artistic life. By advocating, you are ensuring that this right is embedded into the adolescents' life and thereby supporting a stronger society.

References

Bartlett, S. (2023) *The Diary of a CEO: The 33 Laws of Business and Life*. London: Ebury Press.
Bateson, P. and Martin, P. (2013) *Play, Playfulness, Creativity and Innovation*. Cambridge, UK: Cambridge University Press.
Csikszentmihalyi, M. (1990) *Flow: The Psychology of Optimal Experience*. New York: Harper & Row.
Gee, J.P. (2013) *The Anti-Education Era: Creating Smarter Students through Digital Learning*. New York: Palgrave Macmillan.
Gill, T. (2014) *The Benefits of Children's Engagement with Nature*. London: Greater London Authority.
Jarvis, P., Newman, S. and Swiniarski, L. (2014) *On Becoming an Effective Teacher: A Developmental Approach to Classroom Management*. London: Routledge.
Kolb, D.A. (2014) *Experiential Learning: Experience as the Source of Learning and Development*. 2nd edn. Upper Saddle River, NJ: Pearson Education.
Pellegrini, A.D. (2013) *Play*. 2nd edn. Oxford: Oxford University Press.
Resnick, M. (2017) *Lifelong Kindergarten: Cultivating Creativity through Projects, Passion, Peers, and Play*. Cambridge, MA: MIT Press.
Roffey, S. (2012) Pupil wellbeing and the role of social and emotional learning. In: S. Roffey (ed.) *Positive Relationships: Evidence Based Practice across the World*. Dordrecht: Springer, pp. 19–30.
Sutton-Smith, B. (1997) *The Ambiguity of Play*. Cambridge, MA: Harvard University Press.
Vygotsky, L.S. (1978) *Mind in Society: The Development of Higher Psychological Processes*. Cambridge, MA: Harvard University Press.
Whitton, N. (2018) *Play and Learning in the Higher Education Classroom: A Practical Guide*. Abingdon: Routledge.

Chapter 8

Do we grow out of play or is it taken from us?

My husband works in residential care, supporting young people. One evening, he came home and told me he had spent his evening building a Lego Spider-Man and had an enjoyable evening with one of the service-users, and it had been a positive activity, led by the young person, to spark conversation and do something as a team. I realised that Lego play had not been part of our routine for a considerable amount of time, even though it had featured heavily for several years. I took to the internet, looking at the new kits, and placed an order for a couple of small sets that would get to us by Sunday. Sunday proved a lazy day, and late afternoon I texted my 14-year-old daughter to ask, 'Do you want to come and build Lego with me?' She did and we sat for an hour building designs before I transitioned to cooking dinner, and she returned to binge-watching a TV show.

She would have sat all afternoon watching television, and there was nothing wrong with that. I could have got on with other things that needed doing. My reflective question from this is how often do we ask teenagers to play? We get on with routine and forget to ask; that period seems over. It is not over; it's just not factored into our life anymore, and it is easy to be distracted with the daily tasks in front of us whilst the younger of the clan entertain themselves independently. We had enjoyed a lovely hour, creating and chatting, and sitting in silent concentration, ending with satisfaction that we had made something side by side. It was a reminder that investing in activities such as this brought us not only time together but also a period of calm, relaxation, and creativity. It was also something that we both enjoy doing. Playfulness is something for any age. In fact, when you look at the age recommendations on the Lego website, they advertise their kits for all stages of life, and there are Lego sets specifically targeted for the teenage and adult years.

Societal expectations and play: A cultural construction

Society's view of play as a childish activity deeply impacts how individuals engage with play as they grow older. As people mature, the focus shifts from imaginative exploration to the pursuit of more structured, achievement-oriented activities. This transition is rooted in societal norms that often undervalue play in adulthood. The concept of childhood itself as a social construct demonstrates that there can be significant variations of how childhood is experienced across different cultures and historical periods. In many modern industrialised societies, adulthood is equated with responsibility, seriousness, and productivity, leaving little room for playful behaviour (Mintz, 2004). The stereotype that play is for children reinforces the idea that adults should abandon unstructured, spontaneous activities in favour of more-mature pursuits. However, research suggests that play continues to be critical for personal and social development, beyond childhood. Brown (2009) argues that play is not merely a childhood pastime but a fundamental human behaviour that develops creativity, emotional wellbeing, and social connection throughout life. Nevertheless, many adults face cultural and social pressures to prioritise career goals and family responsibilities, relegating play to the periphery of their lives. This shift is especially prevalent in Western societies, where adulthood is characterised by individual success and productivity (Chudacoff, 2007). In contrast, indigenous cultures, such as the Tsimane people of the Bolivian Amazon, maintain play as a lifelong activity, integrating it into their daily routines and communal practices (Reyes-García et al., 2010). For those of us in Western society, it is worthwhile reflecting on what makes us happy. Do we place too large an emphasis on our salaries and material items and neglect to see the wider community of people around us who can contribute effectively to our wellbeing? Reyes-García's (2024) study on happiness within the Bolivian Amazon found that social relations were key to feeling happy and are embedded into the daily routine. Leisure activities with a social component brought more happiness than independent activities, and a reciprocal kindness is clearly contributes to these good feelings, through the interactions of the group placing a strong emphasis on how sharing leads to a happy environment. Protecting time to be social and share playful activities with others is something we can lose when focused on materialistic objectives.

Whilst the construction of childhood continually evolves, our educational system has remained very similar in design since the Victorian era. As we see artificial intelligence changing how we interact with technology, we need to place more emphasis on being responsive to the purpose of education. Instead of promoting rote learning and hours spent memorising revision notes, we need to adapt the approach so that creativity, problem-solving, and emotional resilience (vital skills for this rapidly changing world) are developed. The traditional approach overlooks the developmental needs of adolescents, who thrive in environments that encourage exploration, collaboration, and innovation. Artificial intelligence and other emerging technologies are transforming the nature of work, requiring a workforce that can think critically and innovate. Educational systems must evolve to reflect this shift by embedding opportunities for adolescents to engage in play that develops these competencies. Play is not merely a break from academic activities but a powerful tool for learning and personal growth. It should also be considered that artificial intelligence is being used by young people so that they can get more play time! I will not say which of my children, but I know they have used it with homework so they can speed up the process and get outdoors with their friends. Our responsibility is to blend the two effectively so that learning is a task that is enjoyed, with the process of learning something they want to engage in as they see its purpose.

Educational structures and the decline of play

The education system plays a pivotal role in shaping individuals' attitudes towards play as they age. Early childhood education is generally play-based, as seen in the Reggio Emilia approach, which emphasises child-led, exploratory learning (Edwards et al., 2011). Play in early education is recognised for its ability to enhance cognitive, social, and emotional development (Pellegrini, 2009). However, as children progress through the school system, the structure of their education changes dramatically. Formal schooling prioritises academic achievement, standardised testing, and rigid curricula, particularly in countries like the United States and the United Kingdom. This educational shift results in a sharp decline in the time allocated for free play or creative activities as children age (Ginsburg, 2007).

In Finland, however, where the educational system adopts a different approach to testing, children continue to engage in play with opportunities for independent research, and research project-based learning is prioritised. Finnish schools recognise that play is integral to learning, and they offer longer break periods and incorporate playful learning into their curricula (Hyttinen et al., 2019). This approach contrasts sharply with the high-stakes testing cultures of other countries, where play is often viewed as a distraction from academic achievement. The global differences in educational systems highlight how policy decisions can either sustain or stifle the role of play in children's and adolescents' lives.

Cultural norms and gender expectations in play

Cultural perceptions of play are also closely linked to gender norms. From an early age, children are often socialised into gender-specific forms of play, which can influence their attitudes towards play as they mature. In Western cultures, boys are generally encouraged to engage in competitive, physical activities, while girls are often directed towards more structured, less spontaneous forms of play, such as role-playing or organised games (Blakemore & Centers, 2005). As these children transition into adolescence and adulthood, these gendered expectations continue to shape how they engage with leisure and play. The cultural construction of gender and play also manifests in adult leisure activities. Men are often encouraged to engage in competitive sports, which align with societal notions of masculinity, while women may participate in more social or aesthetic activities, such as dance or yoga, which are often seen as more feminine (Wood & Eagly, 2002). The pressure to conform to these gender norms can further limit the forms of play that adults feel are socially acceptable, thereby narrowing the range of playful activities available to them.

This is why role models are so important. Exposing children to role models they can relate to across the various sports can be effective; the Women's World Cup in 2023 inspired many females to see the sport as open to them, and a record 46.7 million viewers in Britain watched (Sky Sports, 2024). A year on from the England team making the quarter finals in the 2019 tournament saw 850,000 more committed females than there had been previously within the United Kingdom (The FA, 2019). Role models matter. In 2024, I was fortunate to be a spectator at some of the Paris Olympics with my family. The 2024 Olympics were the first to achieve full gender parity, and the Paris hashtag #GenderEqualOlympics trended around the globe. When we returned to Northern Ireland, a welcome-home event for participating athletes was organised by the Department for Communities and attended by a wealth of children and young people, who could see that people like themselves can go on to achieve gold. Not only did they see that an exciting goal was open to them, but they also saw that these were activities they could do in their daily lives if they wanted to. As professionals, we need to be aware of the language we use and our unconscious responses as to what males and females should do. I am sure all of us have done it at some point, but what is important is to recognise that response and do something positive with it. Do not be afraid to challenge the status quo as an advocate for our younger peers.

Cross-cultural research demonstrates that gender norms are not universal. In some indigenous cultures, such as those in Papua New Guinea, there is less division between male and female forms of play, and the two genders engage equally in playful activities throughout their lives (Burridge, 1969). This suggests that societal constructs around gender play a significant role in determining how long play is sustained into adulthood. Building on this, educational and community initiatives that emphasise inclusivity and the dismantling of gender stereotypes can make a tangible difference. For instance, campaigns that highlight diverse role models from different cultural backgrounds, be they athletes, artists, or innovators, help to normalise participation in a wider variety of activities for all genders. If we integrate policies that promote mixed-gender participation in schools and local organisations, this can further erode the barriers created by traditional gender norms.

Psychological development: Play and cognitive shifts

From a psychological perspective, the decline of play in adulthood can also be understood through the lens of cognitive development. Jean Piaget's theory of cognitive development suggests that, as children grow, their cognitive processes evolve from concrete, hands-on learning to more abstract, logical reasoning (Piaget, 1952). By adolescence, individuals have generally reached Piaget's formal operational stage, where individuals think abstractly and solve problems systematically. This cognitive shift often corresponds with a decline in interest in imaginative or exploratory play, which is more characteristic of the earlier pre-operational and concrete operational stages of development. However, more recent psychological research suggests that play is crucial for maintaining creativity, problem-solving skills, and emotional regulation well into adulthood. According to Stuart Brown (2009), play not only is beneficial for children but is a key factor in adult wellbeing. Brown's research shows that adults who engage in playful activities, whether through sports, hobbies, or creative outlets, tend to be more resilient, better problem-solvers, and have healthier interpersonal relationships.

As explored within Chapter 4, play has been shown to mitigate stress and improve mental health in adulthood. A study by Bateson and Martin (2013) found that play has a profound impact on reducing stress and increasing cognitive flexibility in adults. However, despite these benefits, cultural attitudes and social structures often prevent adults from embracing play. In many cases, the pressures of work and societal expectations push play to the margins of adult life.

Work–life balance and the economic context of play

The modern emphasis on productivity and work is perhaps one of the most significant reasons why play declines as individuals transition from childhood to adulthood. The Industrial Revolution and the subsequent rise of capitalism have had a profound impact on how time is valued. The notion of "time is money" has increasingly influenced Western societies, leading to the prioritisation of work over leisure (Thompson, 1967). In contemporary society, adults are often expected to dedicate much of their time to work, with little opportunity for play or recreational activities. I recently had someone share with me why they were turned down for a job: when offered two options – (1) "Do you prefer to work in an environment that is 9-5 with dedicated downtime?" or (2) "Do you like to work in an environment where you can communicate with your team 24/7?" – they went with the first option and with clear, good reasons behind it. The feedback was this was not what they were looking for. The emphasis on being a workaholic is real.

The cultural value placed on work is particularly pronounced in countries such as Japan and South Korea, where long working hours and intense societal pressure contribute to work-centric lifestyles (Kim, 2016). In these contexts, there is little room for play in adult life, and the lack of leisure time is linked to high levels of stress and burnout (Choi et al., 2013). In contrast, Scandinavian countries like Denmark and Sweden prioritise work–life balance and maintain shorter working weeks, allowing adults more time for play and leisure (Gornick & Meyers, 2003).

Global perspectives on the lifespan of play

While the decline of play in adulthood is a common phenomenon in many industrialised societies, cross-cultural research reveals that not all societies follow this trajectory. In many indigenous cultures, play remains an integral part of daily life, even for adults. For example, among the Ju/'hoansi people of southern Africa, adults regularly engage in playful activities such as singing, dancing, and storytelling, which are viewed as essential for maintaining social bonds and community cohesion (Blurton Jones, 1993). Similarly, in many African and South American indigenous communities, play is seen as a lifelong activity that builds community relationships and survival skills (Weisner, 2002). These global perspectives suggest that the decline of play is not inevitable but is heavily influenced by cultural, societal, and economic factors. Societies that place a high value on community, leisure, and social connection tend to support play throughout the lifespan, whereas those that prioritise individual achievement and productivity often marginalising play in adulthood.

Growing into play

Play clearly evolves as we move out of childhood. As educators, we have the influence to ensure that it is something that remains during the adolescent years. Throughout this book, we see the influence that play has on brain development and social and emotional experiences. When reviewing educational policies from across the globe, playful learning for young people in their secondary school period of learning does not get mentioned, and yet we frequently hear the need for opportunities that promote creativity, inquiry, and creative critical thinking. All of these are related to playfulness, and we require that more policymakers recognise the value of play when writing curriculums and policies. You may have this influence. If you do, remember that language matters; practitioners will follow your lead. For educators and practitioners, evaluate how you can build these skills through a playful pedagogical approach. We need to keep play alive for all stages of life.

References

Bateson, P. and Martin, P. (2013) *Play, Playfulness, Creativity and Innovation.* Cambridge, UK: Cambridge University Press.

Blakemore, J.E.O. and Centers, R.E. (2005) 'Characteristics of boys' and girls' toys', *Sex Roles*, 53(9–10), pp. 619–633.

Blurton Jones, N. (1993) 'The lives of children in different cultures: The Ju/'hoansi', in P.H. Leiderman, S.R. Tulkin and A. Rosenfeld (eds.) *Culture and Infancy: Variations in the Human Experience.* New York: Academic Press, pp. 299–331.

Brown, S. (2009) *Play: How It Shapes the Brain, Opens the Imagination, and Invigorates the Soul.* New York: Avery.

Burridge, K.O.L. (1969) *Tangu Traditions: A Study in the Way of Life, Mythology and Developing Experience of a New Guinea People.* Oxford: Clarendon Press.

Choi, S.L., Goh, C.F., Adam, M.B. and Tan, O.K. (2013) 'The impact of human resource management practices on firm performance in a highly regulated emerging market', *International Journal of Human Resource Management*, 24(5), pp. 905–925.

Chudacoff, H.P. (2007) *Children at Play: An American History*. New York: New York University Press.

Edwards, C., Gandini, L. and Forman, G. (2011) *The Hundred Languages of Children: The Reggio Emilia Experience in Transformation*. 3rd edn. Santa Barbara: Praeger.

Ginsburg, K.R. (2007) 'The importance of play in promoting healthy child development and maintaining strong parent-child bonds', *Pediatrics*, 119(1), pp. 182–191.

Gornick, J.C. and Meyers, M.K. (2003) *Families That Work: Policies for Reconciling Parenthood and Employment*. New York: Russell Sage Foundation.

Hyttinen, T., Juutinen, J. and Krokfors, L. (2019) 'Playful learning environments: Towards a pedagogy of play in early childhood education', *Learning, Culture and Social Interaction*, 21, pp. 278–289.

Kim, S. (2016) 'Long working hours and health in South Korea: Results from the Korea National Health and Nutrition Examination Survey', *International Journal of Environmental Research and Public Health*, 13(6), p. 562.

Mintz, S. (2004) *Huck's Raft: A History of American Childhood*. Cambridge, MA: Harvard University Press.

Pellegrini, A.D. (2009) *The Role of Play in Human Development*. Oxford: Oxford University Press.

Piaget, J. (1952) *The Origins of Intelligence in Children*. New York: International Universities Press.

Reyes-García, V., Gueze, M., Luz, A.C., Paneque-Gálvez, J., Macía, M.J. and Orta-Martínez, M. (2010) 'Evidence of traditional ecological knowledge system resilience: The case of the Tsimane' in the Bolivian Amazon', *Ambio*, 39(4), pp. 257–265.

Reyes-García, V. (2024) *The Secret of Happiness: Lessons from the Amazon*. London: Zed Books.

Sky Sports (2024) 'Women's World Cup attracts record-breaking viewership', *Sky Sports*, 5 February. Available at: https://www.skysports.com (Accessed: 14 June 2025).

The FA (2019) *Impact of the 2019 FIFA Women's World Cup on Girls' Participation*. London: The Football Association.

Thompson, E.P. (1967) 'Time, work-discipline, and industrial capitalism', *Past & Present*, 38(1), pp. 56–97.

Weisner, T.S. (2002) 'Ecocultural understanding of children's developmental pathways', *Human Development*, 45(4), pp. 275–281.

Wood, W. and Eagly, A.H. (2002) 'A cross-cultural analysis of the behavior of women and men: Implications for the origins of sex differences', *Psychological Bulletin*, 128(5), pp. 699–727.

Chapter 9

The seriousness of play

Play is often associated with early childhood; however, it is also a crucial learning mechanism for adolescents. It provides opportunities for experimentation, risk-taking, and self-discovery, which are essential during this developmental stage. While traditional views may marginalise play as a frivolous activity, research highlights its importance in developing cognitive, social, and emotional development during adolescence (Lester & Russell, 2010). I have had people challenge me because of my focus on play in education, once young people move into post-primary education, and I understand their perspective. With countless pressures with curriculum and organisational requirements, it can be challenging to feel confident in embracing pedagogical strategies that vary from the status quo. It is also relevant to appreciate that the typical Western curriculum is designed towards an end goal that requires students to memorise facts and view knowledge through a standardised lens. However, I know very few teachers who do not embrace the wider curriculum and who consider how to bring learning to life. There is also an awareness that many students are not passing exams and struggle to retain the information required for summative assessments. Play can provide us with a strategy to engage students with curriculum, and play also allows for the individual to have autonomy in their learning experience. Despite its benefits, the role of play in adolescents' learning is often undervalued in formal education systems, which tend to prioritise academic achievement over holistic development. However, there is growing evidence that integrating play into educational contexts can lead to better engagement and motivation among adolescents (Sutton-Smith, 1997). Considering the whole-person and their holistic development can help us to develop capabilities within students that we would not be able to do if we were to focus only on academic success.

International pedagogical approaches

In China, which has been making strides towards reducing the rigidity of its education system, play-based learning methods, including project-based learning, have been introduced to allow students to explore problems creatively.

Sun and Rao (2017) found that play-based learning in Chinese schools helped students move away from rote memorisation and engage in deeper critical thinking and creative problem-solving, improving engagement and academic outcomes. Sun and Rao (2017) argue that this shift is vital in preparing Chinese students to be competitive in a global economy that values innovation over repetition. I recently spent a year working on a consultancy project, alongside my main job role, designing new curriculums to use for teaching early years educators in colleges and universities in China. The brief was very clear that adopting project-based learning to provide students with real-life experiences was important and that the courses were to be underpinned by the Commission on Adult Vocational Teaching and Learning (CAVTL) Principles (2013). These principles encourage a collaborative and contextualised approach, where mistakes are learnt from, and the experience of students is built upon to enhance the learning environment. I found it a joy to design innovative curriculums that drew on the latest evidence and research. Play was very much on my agenda.

This project, however, did reveal the complexities of embedding such approaches in a context where traditional hierarchical relationships between teacher and student often prevail. My previous experience of working with universities in China enabled me to understand the need to balance approaches accordingly and ensure that there was clear training for those delivering, so that we could shift the hierarchical teacher–student dynamic. Educators must balance the introduction of innovative methods with an understanding of local pedagogical traditions and expectations to ensure meaningful and sustainable change (Gu & Wang, 2021), so it was important for me to gain more insight into the settings and job roles, and this brought me an understanding of how the core values of what we do are interlinked globally and supported me to continue to develop projects that drew on playful pedagogical strategies. I was able to train the educators, undertaking a series of sessions online, and I reflected after our first session how the approach might have impacted those who attended. In Session 2, as I sat in my office and was broadcast into a large boardroom, I asked the teachers to reflect on how they had used our first session together and what they had gained from it, and all went quiet. Then I noticed a group of the teachers come close to the camera and dance some puppets they had made in front of it so I could see. It made me happy. We were approaching a shift in pedagogical approaches seriously but with play. As of this writing, China is the second most powerful country in the world (Forbes, 2025) and has committed to developing vocational programmes that draw on collaboration, innovation, and creativity.

Teamwork

The social aspect of play facilitates the development of leadership and teamwork abilities, as seen in group sports or collaborative creative projects (Lester

& Russell, 2010). The ability to collaborate effectively in group settings has long-term implications for success in both personal and professional spheres. Structured group play can reduce disparities in classroom dynamics, creating equitable opportunities for all students to contribute and thrive. The benefits of group play extend beyond skill-building; they challenge entrenched social norms by creating spaces where diverse voices can contribute equitably. This is highly important, and, unfortunately, we can find that there are many who go through their school-life shutting their voice down, as they do not feel it is valued. The shared sense of purpose and community that arises from group play can have lasting effects, shaping students' attitudes towards teamwork and collective achievement throughout their lives (Vygotsky, 1978). Play provides us with a mechanism to feel confident in different roles, share our voice, and work as a team – a serious skill required for their adult life.

Disengaged students

In traditional classrooms, adolescents often face pressures related to academic performance, which can negatively impact their self-esteem and willingness to engage in learning (Leone et al., 2020). Incorporating play into the environment offers a powerful counterbalance to these pressures. Strategies such as gamified learning environments and play-based assessments transform challenges into opportunities for personal growth, thereby reducing anxiety and encouraging a positive and engaged approach to education (Deterding et al., 2011). However, the effectiveness of such strategies depends on how well they are integrated into the broader curriculum.

Social justice

It only takes a quick switch-on of the news headlines to see we are living in an era of global complexity and unrest. There is a growing socio-political awareness, and young people are keen to understand how what they are seeing will impact them not just now but in their futures. It is our moral duty to equip young people with the tools to understand, question, and challenge injustice. Social justice education aims not only to develop critical awareness of societal inequalities but also to empower learners to imagine and work towards a more equitable world. Play can be utilised as a serious mechanism for exploring social justice and developing the skills that teens require to ask the big questions and challenge in a productive manner. Using play for serious learning is not a new thing: Huizinga (1938) famously argued that play is a cultural act, one that can both reflect and subvert dominant social norms, and he reminds us that when integrated into educational practice with intentionality and structure, play can bring us a dynamic space for experimentation, dialogue, and agency. Vygotsky (1978) emphasised that learning is deeply social and, mediated by cultural tools (play is one such tool), facilitates peer collaboration within the Zone of Proximal Development, enabling students to construct new understandings together. Play in social justice has the capacity to create experiential learning environments where adolescents can engage in forms of play such as role-play and storytelling, not merely as passive recipients of information about injustice but through understanding of alternative realities that require them to feel, think, and respond from unfamiliar perspectives.

Safe spaces for dialogue

Play can enable the creation of psychologically safe spaces in which teenagers can explore controversial or sensitive topics in a way that feels both protected and empowering. We have seen in Chapter 2 how adolescence is a period of intense identity formation (Erikson, 1968), and play offers a medium through which teenagers can test out roles, beliefs, and values without the fear of making irreversible mistakes. Young people need space to grapple with questions about power, privilege, inequality, and their own positions within these systems. As educators, we have the capacity to develop these spaces so that conversations can take place with ease and humility. Some of you reading may live in diverse towns, whereas others might be in areas where there is little human mobility. For both, it is important that adolescents can feel connected not just with their local area but also with our global citizens. As of this writing, there is much unrest across the globe as some countries are more likely to take on an independent outlook and less likely to work cohesively with other countries' governments. Teenagers need to feel empowered to ask questions on what is going on around them, and as adults, we need to be aware that technology has widened the reach of where future employment can take place. Building safe spaces for dialogue to build empathy will widen the opportunities for adolescents in their future career paths and social relationships.

Collective action

Cultivating social justice education through play is not solely about awareness but also about transformation. Through play, young people can engage in imaginative resistance, envisioning and experimenting with alternatives to the status quo. This process not only encourages creativity and critical thinking but also helps adolescents believe in their capacity to effect change. Game design projects, forum theatre, and youth-led media campaigns are examples of play-based activities that situate teenagers as producers of knowledge and as activists. Teenagers' voices matter, and they have a right to speak up on how their future world and society are shaped. Freire's (1970) notion of praxis, reflection and action directed at the structures of oppression, finds fertile ground in these playful, youth-led interventions, and play can support a sense of collective identity across the teenagers' community circle. Collective action is a powerful and important aspect of humankind. I have worked on some great projects where students have become aware of statistics on domestic violence and have taken collective social action to raise funds to buy resources for the Women's Centre and a project where, to raise the awareness of bullying, they have designed their own social media campaigns. The projects have been brought together through values, playful approaches to the project, and an awareness of the importance of community.

The theory of *flow* in practice

In Chapters 2 and 7, we explored Csikszentmihalyi's (1990) theory of *flow*, but what does this look like in practice when working with adolescents? I spent time with peers to delve into this further. These are small-scale examples but evidenced the value of flow when embedding playful approaches to adolescent learning and formalised social environments.

Enhancing engagement and academic achievement through *flow*: In a secondary school science class, a teacher implemented a project-based learning initiative with students ages 14 and 15. This particular group was disengaged and had been noted as underachieving against national score averages. Principles of the project aligned with those of the *flow* theory, and the educator structured tasks that balanced high challenge with high skill levels. Students worked in small groups to design and test eco-friendly energy solutions, such as solar-powered models and wind turbines. The teacher and the teaching assistant scaffolded these activities by offering differentiated instruction, regular feedback, and opportunities for student autonomy. Classroom observations and student feedback (gained throughout the project and at the end) revealed heightened levels of concentration, enjoyment, and time-on-task which would be seen as hallmarks of *flow*. End-of-term assessments showed statistically significant improvements in science attainment scores compared with the group's semester one results. There was also some feedback from students to report increased interest in science careers, suggesting broader developmental impacts on self-concept and future orientation.

Promoting social development through *flow*-based drama workshops: A youth centre piloted a ten-week drama workshop series for adolescents 14 to 16 years of age who were identified as at risk of social exclusion. Participants were referred through local schools and youth services and had experienced challenges such as low self-esteem, behavioural difficulties, or limited peer relationships. Workshop facilitators designed improvisational theatre activities to create immersive experiences with clearly defined goals and immediate feedback. Activities included devising short scenes based on personal narratives, role-switching exercises, and collaborative script-writing. The programme adopted a *flow*-friendly environment by allowing participants to lose self-consciousness in performance while progressively mastering new skills. Qualitative data from focus groups and facilitator journals indicated improved peer relationships, increased confidence, and greater emotional regulation among participants. Participants also demonstrated positive engagement (not initially – these reports came in from week 5) outside the sessions, as reported by key workers. The flow-based approach was found to provide a safe and immersive space for teenagers to develop social and emotional competencies.

Developing digital literacy and motivation through gamified learning: In a Further Education College ICT (Information and Communication Technology) classroom, a gamified learning module was introduced to address low student motivation and uneven digital literacy levels. This was predominantly with students 16 and 17 years of age. The module was designed around *flow* theory principles to encourage active and sustained engagement. In this module, students progressed through a series of digital design challenges in an online platform that awarded points, badges, and progression levels on the basis of mastery. Tasks required increasingly complex skill applications, including coding interactive stories and building basic websites. The teacher used analytics to adapt challenges in real time, maintaining the optimal balance between difficulty and skill level. Digital portfolio assessments indicated a marked improvement in both technical skills and creative output. Surveys conducted pre- and post-intervention showed significant increases in students' intrinsic motivation and confidence in using digital tools. Students consistently reported feelings of deep focus and satisfaction, indicating that *flow* was achieved.

Why so serious?

My journey in education began in Early Years. I have been subjected to the line 'So you just play all day?' and it drives me to despair. I am sure many of you readers of this book will have had to endure similar responses when asked about your working role. Solidarity, my friend. Since the beginning of my career, I have had the privilege of working across age groups and found that the underpinning values of play and community have been core to developing an environment that develops individuals' holistic progression. Play is an innate need within all of us. It is serious. It is essential. Its power cannot be overlooked.

References

Commission on Adult Vocational Teaching and Learning (CAVTL) (2013) *It's About Work*.... London: Learning and Skills Improvement Service.

Csikszentmihalyi, M. (1990) *Flow: The Psychology of Optimal Experience*. New York: Harper & Row.

Deterding, S., Dixon, D., Khaled, R. and Nacke, L. (2011) 'From game design elements to gamefulness: Defining "gamification"', *Proceedings of the 15th International Academic MindTrek Conference*, pp. 9–15.

Erikson, E.H. (1968) *Identity: Youth and Crisis*. New York: W. W. Norton.

Forbes (2025) *The World's Most Powerful Countries in 2025*. Available at: https://www.forbes.com (Accessed: 14 June 2025).

Freire, P. (1970) *Pedagogy of the Oppressed*. Translated by M.B. Ramos. New York: Herder and Herder.

Gu, M. and Wang, L. (2021) 'Reforming teacher education in China: Challenges and innovations', *Teaching and Teacher Education*, 103, p. 103342.

Huizinga, J. (1938) *Homo Ludens: A Study of the Play-Element in Culture*. London: Routledge & Kegan Paul.

Leone, P.E., Krezmien, M.P., Mason, L.H. and Meisel, S.M. (2020) 'Organising schools to meet the needs of all students: The importance of equity and school climate', *Children and Schools*, 42(1), pp. 7–14.

Lester, S. and Russell, W. (2010) *Children's Right to Play: An Examination of the Importance of Play in the Lives of Children Worldwide*. The Hague: Bernard van Leer Foundation.

Sun, J. and Rao, N. (2017) 'Play-based learning in kindergartens in China: Perspectives of practitioners and young children', *Teaching and Teacher Education*, 63, pp. 64–74.

Sutton-Smith, B. (1997) *The Ambiguity of Play*. Cambridge, MA: Harvard University Press.

Vygotsky, L.S. (1978) *Mind in Society: The Development of Higher Psychological Processes*. Cambridge, MA: Harvard University Press.

Chapter 10

Play in the classroom

Play can provide us with a connection. Traditionally in the classroom, we sit in rows, facing the front, and a lot of time is spent sitting down. I generally get to work a little early, and one term, one of the students arrived each morning roughly around the same time I did. I would commence my routine, turning things on, opening windows, and putting on lights. One of my favourite things to switch on in the classroom is a large sensory bubble tower. It is higher than me and filled with water, with lights gradually changing the colour of the water and bubbles floating up from the bottom. Our morning routine evolved, and the student liked to stand with me for this part. I would switch it on, and we would place our hands on it on each side and observe the bubbles start to wake up. As this happened, we would chat about what the student had been up to, and she would share some of her ideas with me for lessons or things she thought would be good to do as a class team. This student's needs meant that this type of conversation would sometimes feel challenging for her; however, with the bubbles between us, the conversation flowed, and I was very glad to hear her suggestions each day as to how the student felt we could further enhance what we offer. When we approach play in the classroom, it does not always have to be a set activity; instead, it can be something that underpins the other pedagogical approaches that we adopt. This morning ritual was one that opened space for building in playfulness and recognising its importance for our style of communication. It is important to acknowledge that a playful environment does not need to be all singing and dancing; instead, it can be a secure place to investigate and open up so that it is cohesive for learning.

Flexible thinking

Fisher (1992) highlights that play allows adolescents to approach problems from different perspectives, encouraging flexible thinking. This ability to think critically is particularly relevant for teenagers as they transition to more advanced academic material in subjects such as Physics, Chemistry, and Economics, where rote memorisation alone is insufficient. In subjects like

History and Literature, play-based learning methods such as role-playing historical figures or acting out literary scenes allow students to engage with the material on a deeper level, promoting empathy, comprehension, and critical analysis of the subject matter. A study by Lillard et al. (2013) found that playful approaches that involve pretend play, role-playing, and inquiry-based learning encourage adolescents to think critically, question assumptions, and explore various solutions to problems, all skills that we want to see develop within the classroom environment. This active engagement with content not only supports the development of deeper understanding but also allows adolescents to develop important executive functions such as working memory, cognitive flexibility, and self-regulation (Diamond & Lee, 2011). When we encourage flexible thinking, we support teenagers to develop a crucial skill as it enables them to adapt their understanding, consider alternative viewpoints, and approach problems from multiple angles. This move away from rote memorisation to flexible thinking sharpens students' ability to analyse and investigate which are key to a playful pedagogical approach. Playful pedagogies naturally support the development of flexible thinking by creating environments where exploration, imagination, and trial-and-error are valued.

The debunking of the learning styles myth

I find myself frequently surprised by how often learning styles are discussed in education. I see it on teaching training curriculums and have shuddered when seeing it presented in the syllabus of one particular qualification that I teach. In an extensive survey that evaluated 150 different factors for learning, Professor John Hattie (2012) concluded that matching teaching to learning styles made an insignificant impact. As educators, we should consider students' learning preferences, but it is long overdue to debunk the myth of learning styles to prevent learners from focusing on one way of approaching their studies. Working in vocational education, I have seen students sent to us because they are not viewed as *academic* and would do better in a *hands-on* environment. I will challenge this in every situation where this is said to me. Very often, I have seen the same student move into the classroom and find a space where they can explore knowledge in a safe environment, where failure and mistakes are embraced, and continue to work to an incredibly high standard: both academically and hands-on. Many of us, whether in or out of education, can often find ourselves labelling children (I am sure many of us have even done it with our own children) as 'not academic'. This, along with learning styles, is a myth. Very often, it is due to young people moving at their own rate of development and not recognising the value and purpose of education. Reflecting on Chapter 9 and the seriousness of play, we need to work harder at establishing an environment which connects students with the content and ensures student autonomy.

Examples of play in action

During my exploration of play in the classroom, educators shared their insights into what had worked effectively for them. Read through their lessons below and consider how this could help you in your own classroom. The lesson might need to be adapted to suit your own cohort, but these examples can spark your own curiosity and ideas for playful pedagogical approaches:

Biology:

> In my biology class, I introduced a game-based activity where students acted as different organelles within a cell. Each student was assigned a role, like the nucleus, mitochondria, or ribosome, and tasked with demonstrating their organelle's function in maintaining cellular processes. Using props and creative movements, students 'interacted' to simulate the production of energy, protein synthesis, and waste removal. This approach not only made the concept of cellular biology tangible but also allowed students to collaborate and problem-solve as a group. By turning a complex topic into an interactive game, the students retained information more effectively and felt more engaged. Some of them did feel a bit daft at first, but they got into it and the threat of studying in silence with a textbook did the job to overcome the initial embarrassment and they are very much used to this style of learning in my classroom as I've been using it a lot to explain some of the more complicated areas. It has worked. By embedding playful learning, students not only grasped key biological concepts but also developed the communication and teamwork skills necessary for scientific studies.
>
> – Ms. H, Biology Teacher, England

Sports:

> To teach teamwork and strategy in physical education, I designed a 'survival island' game where students were divided into small groups and tasked with crossing an imaginary river using only limited resources like planks and ropes. I used this activity in alignment with the National Curriculum for PE. Each group had to plan their moves collaboratively and adapt strategies if something went wrong, such as 'losing' a plank to a simulated current. The activity encouraged leadership, communication, and critical thinking. At the end of the session, students discussed what strategies worked and how they overcame challenges. One student remarked, 'I didn't think we could do it, but working together made it possible!' Incorporating playful problem-solving in sports helped students see the value of cooperation beyond physical skills. By incorporating play, students were able to meet curriculum objectives while building essential life skills.
>
> – Mr. L, PE Teacher, Northern Ireland

English:

For a lesson on Shakespeare's *Macbeth*, I created an escape-room activity where students worked in teams to solve puzzles based on the play's themes, characters, and key events. For example, one clue required them to decode a message written in Elizabethan English, while another involved arranging scenes in the correct chronological order to 'escape' from the witches' lair. This gamified approach brought the text to life and helped students engage with the material in a hands-on way. One student commented, 'I usually find Shakespeare boring, but this made it exciting!' This approach aligns with the UK National Curriculum for English, which encourages the study of literary heritage texts and promotes interpretative skills. Through play, students were able to meet these objectives while developing a newfound appreciation for classical literature.

– Mrs P, English Teacher, England

FE (Further Education) College - Subject Early Years: I draw on my own experiences here. I teach a unit on the social perspectives of childhood, where students have to analyse how childhood is viewed across time, place, and space. This unit is quite different from the units the students are used to and is traditionally a heavy academic syllabus that contains a lot of essays. To incorporate play, students created personas from different eras and found objects to represent different cultural tools. Collages were made, with references to the research the students had undertaken in groups. Displays, incorporating virtual content, presented their findings to their introductory unit to their sociology course. As vocational subject teachers, we can frequently use play to bring other units to life, such as when teaching a unit on children's early literacy development, we make story sacks and role-play storytelling sessions which build confidence before taking the lead on activities, both in college and when out completing their work placements.

Educator self-assessment prompts

Now that you have read through the examples of how play and playfulness have been used in the classroom for different subject areas, my hope is that this has provided you with your own ideas that could be incorporated into your own teaching strategies. Using the questions below will provide you with the opportunity to reflect further on where and how you can integrate playful pedagogy further. Why not reflect independently and with other educators. By sharing your responses with others, you can refine and develop your ideas whilst establishing a play culture with peers.

How does playful pedagogy align with the curriculum you follow?

In the above examples, we have seen that playful learning is not separate from curriculum goals but can be a vehicle to achieve them. Many national curricula value problem-solving, creativity, teamwork, and enquiry-based learning. Consider how a playful task can support core objectives, such as exploring historical empathy in history, applying mathematical reasoning, or developing spoken language skills in English. Use this reflection to strengthen your rationale for using play in lesson planning and assessment.

Which of the case studies in this chapter resonated most with your own teaching style or subject area? Why?

Consider how the structure or intent behind one of the shared activities might align with your own approach to teaching. If you tend to rely on verbal discussion, a role-play activity could complement this. Or if you have not tried technological tools to enhance your sessions, observe a peer who does this. Reflecting on alignment can help identify opportunities to adapt new ideas without losing your pedagogical integrity. If there was a case study you found interesting but felt was not relevant to you, consider why. Maybe it would not suit the student group, or maybe it challenges you because the style is very different from your own. Why not be brave and challenge that thinking by trying something new to see what happens?

Think of a recent lesson you taught. How could a playful element have been incorporated?

Reflect on a topic that learners found difficult, disengaging, or overly abstract. Could a project, game, simulation, or team challenge have supported better understanding or enjoyment? Identifying specific opportunities for play can help build confidence in planning similar approaches in the future.

Are there current misconceptions in your subject that students find challenging? Could play help address these?

Misconceptions are often rooted in rote learning or superficial engagement. Play allows learners to experiment, fail, and try again, critical for reshaping misunderstandings. Challenge your thinking in how certain topics can be approached as often when we see an area as challenging, we end up approaching it formally rather than playfully. Trust in the students to experiment with ideas and experiences so that they can figure out challenging areas as a team.

What barriers might you face when implementing play? What creative solutions could help overcome them?

Time pressures and physical space limitations are common concerns for educators. However, small adjustments like using quick starter activities, adapting tasks to desk-based formats, or involving students in the design of projects can maintain a playful ethos even within constraints. Reflecting on barriers constructively can lead to more sustainable, embedded approaches.

Once you have reflected on these questions, make sure to return to them once you have begun to adopt more-playful strategies in your pedagogical approach. Evaluate how your perspective shifted once you have implemented different strategies and learn from these. Gain feedback from the students and remember that it might take time for the class to engage actively in what you are hoping to achieve. The adolescents you are working with have been in a school system that has not changed in its overall design for over 100 years, so unpacking the hierarchy and conformity can take time. However, it is well worth it once you see the spark and energy come alight.

References

Diamond, A. and Lee, K. (2011) Interventions shown to aid executive function development in children 4 to 12 years old. *Science*, 333(6045), pp. 959–964. doi: 10.1126/science.1204529. PMID: 21852486; PMCID: PMC3159917.

Fisher, E. P. (1992) The impact of play on development: A meta-analysis. *Play & Culture*, 5(2), pp. 159–181.

Hattie, J. (2012) *Visible Learning for Teachers: Maximizing Impact on Learning*. London & New York: Routledge.

Lillard, A. S., Lerner, M. D., Hopkins, E. J., Dore, R. A., Smith, E. D., and Palmquist, C. M. (2013) The impact of pretend play on children's development: A review of the evidence. *Psychological Bulletin*, 139(1), pp. 1–34. https://doi.org/10.1037/a0029321

Chapter 11

Using play to engage with the wider community

I recently heard the phrase 'Out of many, one people'. This is the national motto of Jamaica and felt like the perfect summary of what a community is. During the years of 13 to 18, adolescents can find themselves sitting on the perimeter, faced with internal changes, while society often places negative stereotypes on the teenage group. As society continues to shift to online interactions, our day-to-day personal communications become less recognisable, and it can be hard for adolescents to strike up conversations with those outside of their friendship and family groups. It is vitally important that organisations that work with young people widen the opportunities for them to interact with the wider community in order to build social support networks and have valuable new experiences. Play can be a powerful tool for this and can connect people who would not typically spend time together. In my role in Further Education, I have seen the many benefits that community projects bring and how learning within intergenerational spaces not just extends knowledge but has a positive impact on teenagers' emotional health.

Informal learning through ecological systems

Bronfenbrenner's Ecological Systems Theory (1979) provides a valuable lens to understand how teenagers grow and learn within the multiple, interconnected layers of their environment. At the heart of the theory is the idea that development does not occur in isolation but is instead shaped by a series of environmental systems, from the immediate settings of family and school to the broader cultural and societal contexts that influence our daily lives.

The microsystem includes the direct relationships that a teenager experiences: family, peers, school, and community groups. The mesosystem represents the interactions between these microsystems, such as a collaboration between a school and a local youth centre. The exosystem includes broader structures that indirectly affect the teenager, such as a parent's workplace or local council policies. The macrosystem reflects the wider cultural values, social norms, and expectations that shape how young people are perceived and treated within society. Bronfenbrenner later added the chronosystem, which

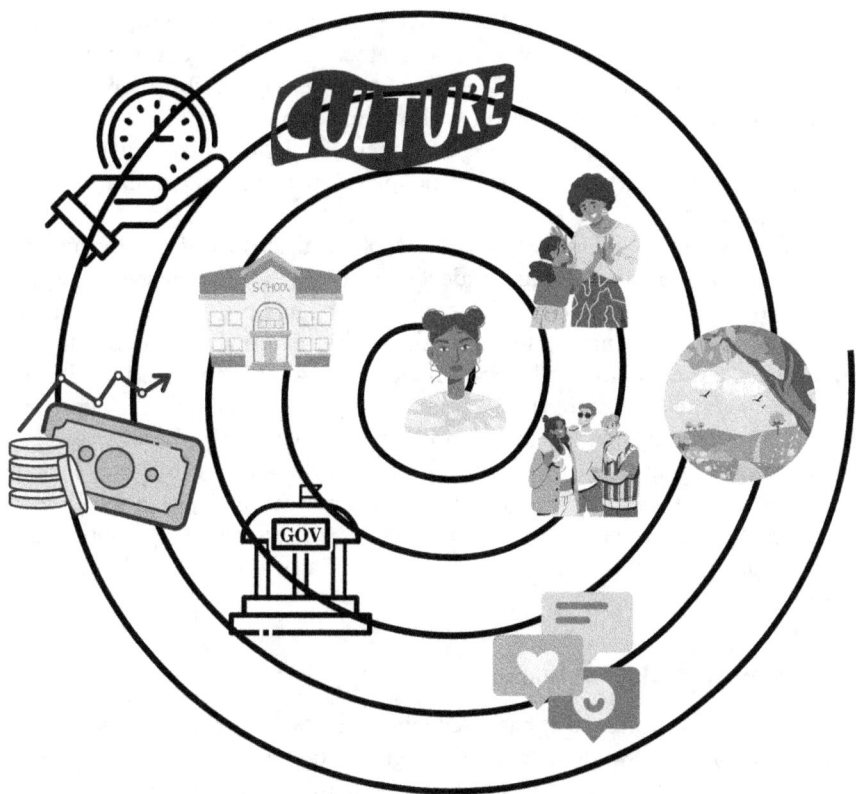

Figure 11.1 Illustrative image of Bronfenbrenner's ecological systems theory. (Created by the author using Canva.)

brings in the dimension of time, acknowledging that these systems change over time and that teenagers' needs and experiences shift during key developmental transitions.

When applied to playful learning and community engagement, Bronfenbrenner's theory offers a practical framework for designing experiences that support teenagers in feeling connected, valued, and involved. Playful projects, especially those that involve community collaboration, have the potential to activate several layers of the ecological model. For example, when teenagers co-create a gardening project with older adults from the local area, they are engaging with their microsystem through direct interpersonal relationships. When this project is supported by their school, a community organisation, and perhaps a local council grant, the mesosystem and exosystem are also engaged.

What makes this particularly powerful for teenagers is that it provides them with a sense of agency within a larger system. They are not just recipients of decisions made elsewhere; they are active participants in shaping their environments. This aligns closely with what teenagers need developmentally: opportunities for autonomy, recognition, and belonging. Bronfenbrenner's model reminds us that connection with society is built not through isolated initiatives but through the weaving together of relationships, organisations, and experiences that support young people to take on meaningful roles in their community.

Designing playful projects using this ecological lens can help ensure that activities are not only engaging but developmentally rich. For instance, organising a community art project that involves teenagers planning a community mural connects the microsystem (student–peer–external attendee relationships), the mesosystem (collaboration between school and community art groups), and the exosystem (local council and public space policy). These initiatives allow young people to see how they fit within the broader societal fabric, encouraging them to contribute in ways that are creative and socially impactful. In this way, play becomes more than recreation, it becomes a bridge between the individual and society, offering teenagers real-world opportunities to explore identity, build networks, and feel part of something bigger than themselves.

Collaborative playful learning

European schools often emphasise collaborative play to enhance social skills and teamwork. In Sweden, schools integrate cooperative games and group projects into the curriculum to encourage students to work together towards shared goals. Samuelsson and Carlsson (2008) highlight the role of play in developing communication, negotiation, and conflict-resolution skills, which are essential for both academic and personal success.

In the United Kingdom, outdoor adventure education, which incorporates physical play and teamwork in natural settings, has been shown to improve social cohesion and leadership skills among teenagers. Dillon et al. (2006) argue that such experiences help students develop trust, communication, and problem-solving abilities in a collaborative environment. This is particularly important in developing a sense of community and belonging, which can positively impact on the social isolation that many adolescents experience during this developmental period.

Collaborative play, when supported intentionally, becomes a co-created form of learning. It empowers teenagers to step into roles that are not always visible within a formal classroom context: planners, leaders, problem-solvers, and compassionate community members. Theories of symbolic interactionism (Blumer, 1969) help us to understand how these interactions support meaning-making and self-identity through social exchanges. When teenagers participate in a gardening session with older adults or rehearse a Christmas performance for a shared audience, they are engaged in more than the act of play; they are actively negotiating roles, responding to others' cues, and reshaping how they are perceived and how they perceive themselves.

At our college, we've observed how collaborative learning environments rooted in playful engagement can support teenagers' connection to their local environment. Activities such as shared storytelling sessions, co-designed seasonal fairs, or games-based art installations can draw young people into more-meaningful relationships with community members. One example involved a pop-up play session set up in a local park, where students invited older residents to share games from their childhood. The students recorded these stories and re-created the games, which were then played together in a celebratory event. What began as a creative writing project evolved into a living museum of intergenerational play and cultural exchange.

Intergenerational communities

In my book *Intergenerational Practice in Schools and Settings* (2023), I have written extensively about the benefits of intergenerational learning. Since writing this book, we have continued as a department to engage with different intergenerational projects and are currently engaged in a pilot, with ten other organisations across the United Kingdom, to evaluate quality intergenerational indicators for intergenerational learning. These will be published internationally for other settings to use for their own intergenerational educational activities. Usually, we integrate programmes into our curriculum, but for this project, this was an addition to our regular weekly schedule. Through meet-ups with a local senior group, one of the students and I observed the interactions between the two groups of attendees and focused on the learning taking place. What became apparent early on was how quickly many of the students began to feel secure enough in this unfamiliar setting to be playful. Without the pressures of formal assessment or peer judgement, they explored different aspects of their personalities: some became natural facilitators, others storytellers or musicians, and many simply enjoyed the freedom to try something new without fear of failure. The sense of safety created by the shared, informal nature of the sessions allowed students to express themselves with spontaneity and confidence. This was particularly evident in quieter students, who were often the first to build one-to-one connections with older participants. Students also began connecting with people they would not ordinarily meet, those from different cultural backgrounds, older adults with lived experience of different generations, and individuals with a wide range of life stories. The relational benefits of this were significant. Students developed empathy, patience, and a deeper appreciation for the richness of human experience. They reported feeling listened to and taken seriously, which for many was an affirming experience. There was also a noticeable shift in how they viewed themselves and each other; working across generations seemed to dissolve some of the social labels often present in teenage groups.

Over the years and in various projects, I have always been so encouraged to continue to build on our work in this area, not just because of the unique learning opportunities but because of the positive emotional impact that it has on the young people I work with. They see us educators differently during these sessions, and we see skills shared that we have not seen up until that point. Examples of this have been one of the team members leading an Irish dancing session, something she had not done for a while and thoroughly enjoyed. We have seen students bring in flutes and whistles, leading music performances for those in attendance. Another member of the team brought in musical friends to lead the Christmas performance, and students have sung us an array of different tunes. This would not have happened unless we had created a playful environment where individuals felt safe to share their hobbies from outside of college.

As reported in written and interview feedback, the time in college to interact with senior members from our community, while engaging in playful activities, has been the most impactful. Where life can be very isolating, across generations, the opportunity to connect with people in the college environment brought a new space to learn and share conversation with people they might not meet in their typical interactions.

Outdoor spaces

In our college, we are fortunate to have a large, green, outdoor space. The garden consists of a typical grass playing field, a polytunnel, and a garden that includes sitting spaces and sensory elements. Over the past three years, I have been working with the team to evaluate how we ensure that this becomes a sustainable space and an extension to our indoor classroom environment.

One of the Biology lecturers had previously taught a unit on environmental studies within the classroom, and the polytunnel and extended garden provided a space to bring the learning objectives to life through practical activities, designed to enhance the curriculum. The polytunnel now hosts an array of vegetables from carrots, tomatoes, and aubergines to pumpkins and sweet fruits that can be used by not only the hospitality students but also staff and students. Muddy paths and squelching patches have proven beneficial for the Early Years students, inviting young children from the local nurseries to come over to the garden to be participants in the activities that students have planned for their portfolios. The garden space has brought the textbooks to life and involved students in creating a learning space that is utilised across vocational areas, developing a college community that respects each other's work and gets to know different students from other courses.

Learning walks

I have found learning walks an increasingly valuable tool, not only for physical movement but as a space for reflection, exploration, and community connection.

We have found that taking learning outside the classroom provides students with space to engage with their thoughts, their environment, and each other in more meaningful ways. These walks are often used during tutorial sessions, providing a calmer and less formal setting for students to reflect on their progress, discuss future plans, or explore topics connected to personal development. There is something powerful about walking side-by-side rather than sitting face-to-face as it reduces pressure and opens up opportunities for more open, honest conversation. Students have shared that they feel more at ease when outside, free from the classroom walls, and I have observed that the conversation flows much more easily. Other tutors using learning walks have also observed a shift in dynamic: conversations become more personal, more purposeful, and often more productive. Difficult topics such as anxiety, future aspirations, or feelings of isolation have been easier to address when walking together, often in green or familiar community spaces.

In addition to reflection, we have used local walks as opportunities to explore the wider community and build social confidence. For example, a mapped walk through the town centre encouraged students to stop at key community landmarks: a library, café, and local heritage site. At each stop, students were encouraged to initiate a conversation, ask a question, or simply observe how the space was being used. These experiences often led to powerful moments of discovery, students learning about spaces they had not previously accessed, striking up conversations with local residents, or seeing their town through a new lens. Such practices can actively break down the segregation that can exist between young people and the broader community. Teenagers are often met with suspicion or discomfort by others. Learning walks allow them to take up space in a positive, visible way and to practice the kinds of informal social interactions that are essential for life. Through their walks, they begin to see their role in the community differently, not as passive observers but as participants with something to offer and something to learn.

Social play and community cohesion

Tribal societies are often characterised by a strong sense of community, where social ties and collective identity are paramount. Play is one of the mechanisms that support this cohesion among teenagers, helping them learn the social rules and responsibilities of the group. Through play, adolescents experiment with social roles, practice leadership, and strengthen relationships with their peers and elders.

In the Maasai culture of East Africa, for example, play among teenagers includes games like jumping contests and mock battles, which serve not only as physical training but also as social bonding rituals. For boys, these activities prepare them for the physically demanding life of a warrior while reinforcing values such as bravery, endurance, and group loyalty. For Maasai girls, play activities often mimic the roles they will take on as adults, such as learning domestic skills or participating in communal dances. Through these forms of play, teenagers engage with the broader social structure of the Maasai, understanding the roles within the community and the responsibilities they will eventually assume. In the Trobriand Islands of Papua New Guinea, adolescent play often centres on yam exchanges, which are a crucial part of the local economy and social structure. Teenagers participate in yam festivals and mock exchanges, learning the complex rules of reciprocity and gift-giving that underpin Trobriand society. These playful activities teach the importance of social relationships, economic exchange, and the role of status within the community. What we see in these examples of play is how it is a central mechanism for passing on cultural knowledge, building social bonds, and preparing young people for adult roles. Western educational systems often compartmentalise learning and overlook the value of informal, social, and embodied experiences. By recognising the significance of play as a developmental and communal tool, we can begin to rethink how teenagers engage with their communities. There is much to learn from cultures where play is woven into daily life and where teenagers are trusted to take on meaningful roles through shared activity.

Reflection

I now invite you to pause and reflect on your own setting. How are the teenagers you work with currently connecting with their local community? Are there opportunities for them to play, explore, and interact with people beyond their usual circles? If not, what might be possible if they did? Too often, community engagement for teenagers is positioned as something formal or structured, volunteering hours, civic participation, or school trips with a clear educational outcome. However, we can re-frame these experiences through a playful lens. Why not integrate a lunchtime music session in a public park, a co-designed mural with older residents, or a storytelling walk through town to become meaningful moments of belonging for young people.

Play invites freedom, experimentation, and relationship-building. It softens boundaries and creates shared experiences where stereotypes and social divides begin to dissolve. Consider how your role, your environment, and your partnerships might support this. What outdoor or community spaces are available nearby? With whom could you collaborate to make playful learning possible beyond the classroom? What stories do your students want to tell, and where might those stories be shared?

References

Blumer, H. (1969) *Symbolic Interactionism: Perspective and Method*. Englewood Cliffs, NJ: Prentice-Hall.

Bronfenbrenner, U. (1979) *The Ecology of Human Development: Experiments by Nature and Design*. Cambridge, MA: Harvard University Press.

Cole, F. (2023) *Intergenerational Practice in Schools and Settings*. Abingdon: Routledge.

Dillon, J., Morris, M., O'Donnell, L., Rickinson, M. and Scott, W. (2006) *Engaging and Learning with the Outdoors – The Final Report of the Outdoor Classroom in a Rural Context Action Research Project.* Slough: National Foundation for Educational Research (NFER).

Samuelsson, I.P. and Carlsson, M.A. (2008) 'The playing learning child: Towards a pedagogy of early childhood', *Scandinavian Journal of Educational Research*, 52(6), pp. 623–641.

Chapter 12

Using technology to play and prosper

As a lecturer in Early Years, I find that my main teaching role is supporting students who are training to work with children and young people. One afternoon, we were exploring how technology can be used playfully to support development. The task was simple: in small groups, students selected an app or online tool and designed an activity that would be suitable for a child to engage with. What followed was an unexpected burst of laughter, competition, and focused discussion as students trialled each other's creations and offered feedback. I glanced at the clock and realised we were 15 minutes past our scheduled finish time. No one, not even me, had noticed. Flow had commenced and we were fully focused on the playful interactions we were engaged with. The most powerful part? They hadn't just been playing; they had been engaging in deep, purposeful learning without even realising it.

This moment was a lovely reminder, as I worked through the creation of this book, that when learners are truly immersed, play can become a powerful teaching tool at any age. Whether it's early years or adolescence, play doesn't mean a lack of structure; it means purposeful, joyful engagement. In this chapter, we will explore how teachers working with adolescents have embraced digital play and gamification to capture attention, ignite curiosity, and develop a range of skills that are essential in both academic and future professional settings.

Moments like these are a reminder that integrating play through technology isn't just adding fluff to lessons; it is a powerful strategy to engage the adolescent mind. In this lesson, gamification had enhanced the learning experience. A colleague of mine is a big fan of Kahoot quizzes (a platform used by over 8 million educators worldwide) to turn routine summative and formative assessment into a playful game that students want to participate in. The instant feedback, competition, and fun of the quiz tap into a natural love of play, and instead of passively jotting down notes, students are proud to share answers, debate accuracy, and actively recall what they learned. Observing interactions of these quizzes leaves me reflecting on how a simple digital tool can transform the classroom atmosphere. In that playful space of the quiz competition, real learning was happening almost effortlessly.

This small anecdote is echoed by teachers across the globe. "I used to struggle to keep my class focused during grammar lessons. Now they actually look forward to them," says Liz, a secondary English teacher in London. "Every Friday, we do a Kahoot! quiz on that week's topics. The class cheer each other on, and I can practically see the knowledge sticking as they play. I've never seen them so alert at 3 o'clock on a Friday!" For Liz, injecting a dose of game-based competition revived a class that used to yawn through parts of speech. The experience is similar for Arjun, a science teacher in New York, who reflects that "using games in class has been a game-changer, literally. Even the shy students come alive during a quiz or a challenge. It's like the gameplay removes their fear of being wrong; they just try, and in trying, they learn." These reflections capture an exciting shift: when we harness adolescents' natural enthusiasm for play, we create learning moments that stick.

Game on: Engaging students through gamification

Educators around the world are discovering that gamified learning can reignite student motivation, especially in subjects that teenagers often find dry or difficult. In recent years, secondary schools in the United Kingdom have increasingly woven game elements into lessons to make learning more interactive and enjoyable. Platforms such as Kahoot! and Minecraft: Education Edition are now commonly used to enliven topics from history to science, turning traditional content into interactive experiences. The appeal of these tools isn't just anecdotal; research supports their impact. Hamari et al. (2016) found that adding gamification significantly boosts student motivation and engagement, particularly in subjects where interest was previously lacking. By incorporating classic game elements like rewards, points, challenges, and instant feedback, schools create a more dynamic, student-centred environment where adolescents are eager to participate.

Consider a typical STEM (science, technology, engineering, and mathematics) class, where concepts like circuits or chemical bonding often appear abstract and disconnected from real life. Priya, a science teacher in Birmingham, England, decided to introduce Minecraft: Education Edition to support students' understanding of electrical circuits. Students were challenged to create a functioning model of a smart home using Redstone, Minecraft's version of wiring. "The change in energy was instant," Priya shared. "Students who usually stayed quiet during theory lessons were now debating where to place switches or how to create logic gates. Some even started watching YouTube tutorials outside class to refine their designs." What emerged was not only deeper content understanding but also evidence of collaboration, resilience, and independent research. Priya's story shows how the immersive nature of Minecraft can help students visualise and manipulate complex systems in a playful way. Instead of passively taking notes, students were actively problem-solving in real time, discovering that science could be both relevant and fun.

Globally, this trend of *learning by playing* is gaining momentum. In The Netherlands, for example, secondary schools have adopted playful, gamified projects to tackle real-world problems in the classroom. The idea is to let students approach complex challenges, like environmental issues or community planning, through game-like simulations or competitions. A study by Gielen et al. (2010) in Dutch schools found that such game-based learning significantly improved students' analytical skills in subjects like mathematics and science. The reason? When students are engrossed in a game scenario, they naturally practice critical thinking and logical reasoning to overcome obstacles. They become *problem-solvers* because the game demands it. One Dutch teacher, Marieke in Rotterdam, attests to this:

> We created a city-building game for our geography class. The students had to 'win' by designing a city that balanced budget, ecology, and happiness. I was amazed. They debated trade-offs, did research on their own, and were so excited to prove their city was the best. It was learning, but it felt like play for them.

This gamified approach provided a low-stakes environment for experimentation, where failing in the game simply meant trying a new strategy, an experience that traditional tests rarely offer.

Even in countries known for intense academic pressure, educators are finding room for play. In South Korea, where high schoolers often face long hours of lectures and exam prep, teachers have turned to gamified platforms to make subjects like Maths and Science more interactive and appealing. Research by Hamari et al. (2014) reinforces this approach: integrating point systems, badges, or challenges into lessons can significantly improve engagement and motivation among teens. The intrinsic motivation sparked by games encourages students to take charge of their own learning. "My students will do extra practice problems voluntarily if it's framed as a game," notes Sun-hee, a secondary math teacher in Seoul, South Korea. "I used an app that turns problem-solving into an adventure quest. I have students staying after class to level up their characters by solving more equations. It still astonishes me!" The popularity of such approaches in South Korea and elsewhere speaks to a universal truth: adolescents everywhere love a good challenge, and if that challenge is presented playfully, they dive in wholeheartedly.

This surge of gamification is not limited to quizzes and academic games; it extends to how teachers manage and inspire students on a broader level. One striking example is *Classcraft*, a platform that transforms classroom behaviour and participation into a role-playing game. In Classcraft, students create characters, join teams, and earn experience points or *powers* by completing assignments, helping classmates, or even just bringing a positive attitude. Nadia, a secondary school teacher in Ottawa, Canada, describes the change after she implemented a Classcraft-style system:

Our class became a little community of warriors and healers. If someone was falling behind, their team would rally to help because their game depended on it. Homework turned into 'quests,' and participation in discussions skyrocketed because everyone wanted to earn points for their character. The shy students started to find their voice.

Nadia's story shows how gamifying the social environment of the classroom can develop collaboration and a sense of belonging. Instead of competing *against* each other for grades, her students began collaborating within teams to achieve shared goals. Research supports this boost in teamwork: game-based learning and class gamification have been noted to cultivate social skills like cooperation and communication (Diaz & Estoque-Loñez, 2024). By turning the classroom into a playful arena, we can often sidestep the apathy, or fear of embarrassment, that hinders participation. In the game, everyone has a part to play.

Playful learning, serious skills

While the fun and engagement of educational games are immediate benefits, the deeper value of playful learning lies in the skills it nurtures. Well-designed games and playful activities naturally encourage critical thinking, creativity, and resilience. Renowned education researcher James Paul Gee (2003) emphasised that good educational games promote exactly these skills – they require learners to adapt to new challenges, experiment with strategies, and learn through trial and error. In other words, playing is *problem-solving*. When a student navigates a complex level in a game or figures out the rules of a new playful task, they are exercising their brain in ways traditional lectures might not. They learn to formulate hypotheses ("Maybe I need to try a different approach to solve this puzzle"), test their ideas, and iteratively improve their methods, which is essentially the scientific method wrapped in fun.

Returning to Minecraft: Education Edition, this is a shining example of a tool that merges play with rigorous skill-building. This sandbox game, widely used by millions of students and teachers in over 100 countries (Slattery et al., 2023), allows adolescents to build and explore virtual worlds. On the surface, it looks like simple block-building. But step into a classroom using Minecraft and you'll see something magical: history students reconstructing ancient civilisations, science students experimenting with virtual electrical circuits, and language students building story settings, all completely absorbed in the task. A teacher from Finland shared with me how in their secondary school history class, they were using Minecraft to recreate a World War I trench. She found the students so engrossed in the task of constructing the terrain and deciding how to place the bunkers that they ended up diving deep into research about trench layouts, soldier life, and battle strategies, far beyond what a textbook alone would prompt. The teacher shared that one quiet student became the unofficial *team leader* because of his Minecraft expertise, gaining confidence as he taught his classmates how to craft artillery or set up supply lines in the game. This collaborative project did more than teach history; it let students experience a bit of the decision-making and problem-solving that historical figures faced. The play created a rich context for learning that no lecture could replicate.

Teachers often report that these kinds of playful, technology-enhanced projects unveil strengths in students that traditional methods do not. "I had a student who struggled with writing assignments but excelled at storytelling in our class podcast project," shares Grace, an English teacher from Fermanagh, Northern Ireland.

> When we switched to a more playful approach, like having students create video diaries for characters in a novel using Flip, he suddenly found his element. He added creative video effects, spoke with confidence as he 'became' the character, and offered insights about the story that he'd never articulated on paper. It was the same literature content, but presented in a way that let him play and experiment. His critical thinking was evident in the video, even though he never wrote a traditional essay on that unit.

Grace's experience with Flip, a video discussion platform, highlights how technology can open alternative pathways for expression. By allowing students to respond with videos, images, or audio in a playful manner, we give those who struggle with conventional assessments an opportunity to shine. Importantly, research has found that using such video-based platforms can improve student engagement, particularly in online or hybrid settings. The act of creation, whether it's building in Minecraft, recording a Flip video, or designing a digital poster, invites students to engage more deeply and think critically about the subject matter because they are actively doing something with their knowledge.

Another key skill area where playful technology makes a difference is problem-solving under new or uncertain conditions. Traditional schooling often presents problems with a single correct answer and a known method. In contrast, games and playful simulations throw students into uncharted territory. They have to *learn how to learn* from the situation. For instance, a game might give only partial information and require players to infer the rest, or it might introduce random events that force students to adjust their strategy. This mimics real life, where problems are rarely neatly packaged. Educational games encourage students to embrace mistakes as part of the learning process: if one approach fails, try another (just as my nail technician friend wipes off a design that isn't working and starts over, as I recounted in Chapter 3). Research from various contexts confirms this advantage. Ramani and Siegler (2008) demonstrated that even simple math and logic games can boost adolescents' numerical reasoning and their ability to apply mathematical principles in novel contexts. In the playful arena of a game, teenagers often push themselves harder than they would with a worksheet, because the process is enjoyable and they want to succeed in the game. As a result, they get comfortable with complexity and uncertainty, invaluable skills for higher-order thinking and real-world problem-solving.

Artificial intelligence gamification

Recent advances in artificial intelligence (AI) are expanding the potential of gamification in education, offering new opportunities for personalisation and inclusion through playful learning. AI-powered platforms can adapt in real time to each student's performance, modifying the difficulty, pace, or even the type of task to suit individual learning needs. This approach creates more equitable learning environments, where students who may struggle in traditional classroom settings can engage in meaningful learning at their own pace and in a way that suits their cognitive or emotional profile.

One example is AI-driven educational games that use adaptive learning algorithms to scaffold challenges. These systems can identify when a student is succeeding easily and introduce more complexity or, conversely, provide support and hints when a learner is struggling. This dynamic responsiveness prevents students from feeling either bored or overwhelmed, common barriers to engagement for both high achievers and those with additional learning needs. Research by Holmes et al. (2019) found that AI-enhanced learning environments improved motivation and participation among students who had previously disengaged from classroom tasks, especially those with diverse learning profiles.

AI gamification often includes multimodal interaction: combining text, visuals, audio, and even gesture-based responses. This can be especially powerful for students with additional learning needs, including dyslexia, attention-deficit/hyperactivity disorder, or sensory processing differences. AI's ability to simplify language, highlight key instructions, or even convert written information into spoken feedback can help students navigate challenges more independently. As noted in a review by Huang and Spector (2021), this integration of AI allows for more Universal Design for Learning (UDL) principles to be embedded into gamified systems, ensuring that accessibility is not an afterthought but a core component of the learning design.

AI-powered gamification can also contribute to cultural and linguistic inclusion. Many platforms now include real-time language translation, voice recognition for diverse accents, and content that can be localised or adapted for different regions. This has particular relevance for classrooms with students from multilingual backgrounds, where understanding academic content in a second or third language can pose challenges. By allowing learners to interact with content in their preferred language and through culturally responsive avatars, AI gamification can create a more welcoming and affirming learning environment.

One of the most powerful aspects of AI-supported playful pedagogy is the ability to gather ongoing, formative data without disrupting the flow of learning. While students are immersed in game-like challenges, AI can track patterns, identify skill gaps, and generate insights for educators. This real-time feedback supports early intervention and more personalised teaching strategies without stigmatising learners. Rather than waiting for a formal test result, educators can be alerted to where a student needs support and address it through further play-based scaffolding.

When thoughtfully implemented, AI gamification not only enhances motivation and engagement but becomes a tool for justice, recognising and responding to the diverse needs of adolescents in increasingly complex and inclusive classrooms. It affirms that play is not a privilege but a powerful pathway through which every young person can access learning and agency. As AI continues to evolve in our learning environments, there are ethical tensions that we need to consider; for example, AI is a large consumer of water and relies on rare minerals (UN Environment Programme, 2024), and as with anything new, we need to ensure that a research-informed approach is adopted. However, AI is a tool we can use in the classroom to support inclusive playful pedagogy.

From play to real-world gains

Sceptics might still wonder: *Is all this fun and play really making a difference in academic outcomes?* The evidence increasingly says yes. Gamified learning is not just about momentary engagement; it can translate into concrete improvements in learning. Karl Kapp (2012), a prominent author on game-based learning, highlighted that making learning more enjoyable through game elements tends to improve students' retention of information. When students are emotionally invested and actively involved in a lesson (as they often are when playing), the content *sticks* better in their memory. This is something many of us have observed anecdotally: think about how a student might forget a formula they memorised by rote, but they will vividly recall a science concept after having *played* with it in a lab simulation or a game.

Empirical research backs up these observations. A meta-analysis from Huang et al. (2020) pulled data from over 3,000 students and found a small to moderate positive effect on learning outcomes when gamified learning was compared with traditional methods. In simpler terms, students who learned with gamified activities tended to perform better, their understanding and test scores improved (with an average effect size indicating notable gains), and more recent research is even more encouraging. A 2023 review of studies involving over 5,000 learners reported an overall large improvement in student learning outcomes with gamified approaches, underlining that when done well, gamification can significantly boost academic performance (Li et al., 2023). These studies suggest that the benefits of playful learning are not just in engagement or soft skills but also in measurable academic achievement.

Beyond test scores, playful technology-enhanced learning contributes to a broader set of outcomes that are vital for the 21st century. Many education systems, from Europe to Asia, are recognising that skills like creativity, collaboration, and adaptability are just as important as content knowledge. Gamified and play-based learning happens to be a terrific way to cultivate these. When students play *together*, be it on a team in a quiz game or co-building a project in a virtual world, they practice communication and teamwork. The competitive element of games can actually bring students together, as we saw in Nadia's Classcraft lesson, where teams collaborated to help each other succeed. Research has noted that these technologies can enhance social and collaborative skills, aligning with goals of improving educational inclusivity and teamwork (Diaz & Estoque-Loñez, 2024). In an increasingly interconnected world, learning how to work (and play) well with others is a critical outcome in itself.

There are also subtler gains. Playful learning often creates a classroom atmosphere of psychological safety, where students feel more comfortable taking risks. In a game, failing doesn't feel so dire, as you can always try again. This attitude can spill over into how students approach non-game tasks, making them more resilient and persistent. One teacher, Michael, who teaches high school biology in Tyrone, Northern Ireland, shared an insightful observation:

> After I incorporated more playful activities, like a digital scavenger hunt for learning cell biology, I noticed my students became less afraid to ask questions or make guesses. The game taught them that sometimes you have to venture a guess to move forward. Now, even in our regular labs, they're more willing to hypothesise or predict an outcome, even if they're not 100% sure. That fear of being wrong has diminished.

Play can be used in lessons to support a cultural shift in attitudes to making mistakes, especially in environments where students are typically exam-conscious and risk-averse. Indeed, in countries like Japan and South Korea that traditionally emphasise high-stakes testing, introducing playful learning has been shown to help students develop a more robust understanding of concepts by allowing them to learn from mistakes in a low-stakes test. Play provides the *freedom to fail*, turning errors into learning opportunities.

It is important to note that technology is not a means to an end. Simply having devices or educational games in a classroom does not guarantee a playful, rich learning experience. It's the thoughtful integration, the pedagogy behind the technology, that matters. The best outcomes occur when teachers facilitate reflection and connections during and after the play. For example, after a lively 'Kahoot!' quiz, a teacher might lead a discussion on why the most-missed question was tricky, turning a fun moment into a critical thinking opportunity. After students design a project in Minecraft, a debrief can help them articulate what they learned and how they solved problems. Technology provides the tools and context for play, but it's the educator who guides students to extract meaning from the experience. This partnership between educator creativity and tech tools is what truly supports playful learning.

References

Diaz, R. and Estoque-Loñez, A. (2024) 'Gamification and collaborative learning: A review of classroom strategies', *Journal of Educational Technology and Society*, 27(2), pp. 58–73.

Gee, J.P. (2003) *What Video Games Have to Teach Us About Learning and Literacy*. New York: Palgrave Macmillan.

Gielen, M., Peeters, L. and De Backer, F. (2010) 'Game-based learning and student analytical skill development in Dutch secondary education', *Educational Research and Innovation*, 15(4), pp. 211–226.

Hamari, J., Koivisto, J. and Sarsa, H. (2014) 'Does gamification work? — A literature review of empirical studies on gamification', *47th Hawaii International Conference on System Sciences*, pp. 3025–3034.

Hamari, J., Shernoff, D.J., Rowe, E., Coller, B., Asbell-Clarke, J. and Edwards, T. (2016) 'Challenging games help students learn: An empirical study on engagement, flow and immersion in game-based learning', *Computers in Human Behavior*, 54, pp. 170–179.

Holmes, W., Bialik, M. and Fadel, C. (2019) *Artificial Intelligence in Education: Promises and Implications for Teaching and Learning*. Boston: Center for Curriculum Redesign.

Huang, B. and Spector, J.M. (2021) 'Adaptive learning with AI: Personalisation and equity', *Educational Technology Research and Development*, 69(3), pp. 143–160.

Huang, W.H., Johnson, T.E. and Han, S.H.C. (2020) 'Gamification in education: A meta-analysis', *Educational Research Review*, 30, p. 100308.

Kapp, K.M. (2012) *The Gamification of Learning and Instruction: Game-Based Methods and Strategies for Training and Education*. San Francisco: Pfeiffer.

Li, Y., Zhang, H. and Chen, M. (2023) 'Gamified learning and student achievement: A meta-analytic review of 5,000 participants', *Journal of Computer-Assisted Learning*, 39(1), pp. 12–30.

Ramani, G.B. and Siegler, R.S. (2008) 'Promoting broad and stable improvements in low-income children's numerical knowledge through playing number board games', *Child Development*, 79(2), pp. 375–394.

Slattery, R., Nguyen, C. and Lund, T. (2023) *Minecraft in the Classroom: Global Trends and Pedagogical Benefits*. Seattle: EdTech Research Lab.

United Nations Environment Programme (2024) *Environmental Impacts of Artificial Intelligence: A Global Review*. Nairobi: UNEP.

Chapter 13

True play
Understanding the difference of play in and out of the classroom

Throughout this book, I have drawn on play-based approaches that can be adopted for educational pedagogy. All good educators that I have observed see teaching as their craft and draw on different strategies to provide students with a well-rounded and developed curriculum. When putting together the research for this book, I was very aware of my playwork background and knew it was important to recognise that the play I write about that takes place in the classroom is different to the uninterrupted and deep play that comes from the individual's own choice. True play is a type of play we see frequently when observing young children but becomes less apparent as we progress into adolescence and adulthood. To create a space for individuals to engage in true play, we need to believe in the art of spontaneity.

Supporting true play in the adolescent environment means providing young people with space to rehearse adulthood symbolically, without judgement or expectation. As one youth mentor in Glasgow noted whilst I undertook my research, "Sometimes the loudest laughter and deepest conversations happen in the spaces between structured activities. That's where real play happens, with inside jokes, made-up games, and weird little rituals only they understand." True play often flourishes in the unstructured, in-between moments we too easily overlook.

The Play Cycle

The Play Cycle offers a powerful lens through which to understand how teenagers initiate, sustain, and complete moments of authentic play. Developed by Bob Hughes (2001), the Play Cycle consists of the *play cue* (an invitation to play), the *play return* (the response), the *play flow* (ongoing mutual engagement), the *play frame* (the physical or emotional container for the play), and finally *play annihilation* (the ending of the episode, either intentionally or through interruption).

In teenage contexts, play cues can be subtle. They might be in the form of sarcastic remark, a knowing glance, or a shared digital image. If a peer responds, the interaction can spiral into a flow of improvisation, humour, or joint

102 Play and Adolescence

Figure 13.1 A photo of an 'invitation to play' at a meeting the author Fey Cole attended. Lego play was used as a tool to plan the strategic vision for an organisation.

creativity. Understanding this process is key to safeguarding space for play to evolve. "Play for teens is about testing limits in a safe space," explained an outdoor education leader in Wales. "They'll push the rules, reframe the activity, or flip the script on a game. We don't shut it down. Instead, we hold the frame and let them stretch inside it." This emphasis on maintaining the play frame without intruding upon it is central to adolescent engagement.

Applying the Play Cycle to real-world context reveals that teenage play is often spontaneous, fleeting, and peer-led but no less meaningful. A youth centre manager from Dublin shared:

> We had a teen who built a cardboard city out of leftover boxes in the hall. Other young people joined in, drawing signs, making characters, filming it like a movie. No one planned it. That's true play: spontaneous, collective, and completely theirs.

This exemplifies how play cues can ignite rich, shared experiences when the environment allows. Yet these cycles can be fragile; they are often broken by adult misinterpretation or intervention. Lester and Russell (2008) argue that young people need space that is free from adult agendas in order to explore and play in ways that reflect their emotional landscapes. The adult role is not to orchestrate the play but to be attuned to its rhythms, to offer time, materials, and safety without co-opting the moment. As a detached youth worker in Northwest England put it, "The moment we let go of 'what are they learning?' and focus on 'what are they exploring?', you start to see genuine play emerge in the jokes, the drama, the quiet tinkering in the corner."

Designing spaces that support true play requires a shift from programmatic thinking to relational and environmental attentiveness. When young people are given ownership over their environments, their willingness to engage playfully increases. "When we added a 'no purpose' zone in the centre, just lights, chalk walls, beanbags, everything changed," shared a youth worker working in Derry/Londonderry. "It gave them permission to just be. That's when you see true play: no judgement, no agenda, just exploration." Creating these kinds of open, responsive spaces allows teens to initiate play cues and sustain them without fear of surveillance or judgement. This means not eliminating all structure but rather recognising when structure serves the young people and when it simply replicates adult control. True play thrives where autonomy, creativity, and community intersect.

Understanding and promoting the Play Cycle in teenage settings challenge the dominant narratives that view adolescent play as trivial or disruptive. Scholars such as Peter Gray (2013) and Stuart Brown (2009) remind us that play is a biological necessity, not just for children but across the lifespan. When teenagers are allowed to play freely, they are not disengaged; they are experimenting, connecting, and learning in deeply embodied ways. A youth arts coordinator in London captured this beautifully:

> Sometimes true play looks like nothing at all, just a group of teens slumped on beanbags, tossing around daft ideas or looping a beat they made. But give it ten minutes and they've created a whole skit or freestyle. That's the magic, we just need to let it breathe.

Creating space for true play in adolescence is not about stepping back entirely; it's about stepping aside and trusting in the Play Cycle, safeguarding the frame, and allowing young people to take the lead in shaping joyful, transformative experiences.

Play across the globe

While adolescence is a universal stage of human development, the ways in which teenagers engage in play vary significantly across different countries and cultures. When we look to our peers across the globe, we can learn so much and offer further opportunities for our young people. It also reminds us that we should challenge our perceptions of play as its significance is valued in different ways across different locations.

Japan: The high value placed on academic achievement and discipline often limits the time teenagers spend on unstructured play. The school system is highly demanding, and many teenagers are involved in *juku* (cram schools) or extracurricular activities that are more structured and competitive than playful. Despite this, Japanese teens still find opportunities for play, often through video games and social media. The gaming industry in Japan is a significant outlet for adolescent play, allowing teens to connect with peers and explore alternative realities where they can exert more control, creativity, and freedom. However, concerns about social isolation and screen addiction have led to debates about the quality of this form of play.

Norway puts a strong emphasis on the value of outdoor play, and physical activity is viewed as an important mechanism for promoting holistic development. Teenagers in Norway often engage in outdoor sports, hiking, and skiing, activities that reflect the country's close connection with nature. The Nordic model of education, which stresses the importance of balanced development and wellbeing, ensures that adolescents have extended time for physical play, even during the school day. Norway's cultural emphasis on a *friluftsliv* lifestyle, living in close connection with nature, shapes the play experiences of teenagers, promoting not only physical health but also emotional wellbeing.

Nigeria: The structure of adolescent play is heavily influenced by communal values and traditional practices. While urbanisation and modernisation have brought about changes, many Nigerian teenagers, particularly in rural areas, engage in play that is deeply rooted in local culture, such as traditional games, dance, and storytelling. These forms of play help to build a strong community cohesion, respect for elders, and the passing down of cultural knowledge. In Nigerian urban areas, access to globalised forms of play, such as football and social media, increasingly influence teenage leisure activities, blending local traditions with modern digital engagement.

Reflect on your own community: How is play valued where you are located? Where are the spaces for teens to play? What do they look like? How much are they utilised? Asking these questions allows for a greater understanding of how to develop play spaces for your locality.

Socioeconomic factors and access to play

Socioeconomic conditions also shape the forms of play available to teenagers. In more affluent societies, teenagers often have access to organised sports, digital technologies, and extracurricular activities that support varied forms of play. By contrast, teenagers in lower-income countries or regions may have limited access to such resources, which affects how they experience play. I must, however, note that the resources required for play do not require costly investment, but the differences between chosen play and play activities will vary greatly depending on accessibility and trends will influence what teenagers may want to engage.

If we look to the United States, socioeconomic disparities are evident in the types of play available to teenagers. Wealthier adolescents may have access to elite sports clubs, private lessons, and expensive gaming systems, while teenagers from lower-income families often rely on community-based resources, public spaces, and free digital platforms for play. Research shows that extracurricular activities such as sports teams are linked to better academic and social outcomes, yet the high cost of participation often limits access for economically disadvantaged teens (Fredricks & Simpkins, 2012). I must stress that community-based resources bring with them a wealth of learning and experiences, but these are often not where governments choose to invest.

In Brazil, football serves as a unifying form of play across socioeconomic classes, particularly in urban areas. Regardless of economic background, many Brazilian teenagers participate in football, either in formal clubs or in informal games on the streets and beaches. The game is deeply ingrained in Brazilian culture and serves as a form of socialisation, competition, and physical exercise. However, while football is accessible to many, other forms of play, such as video gaming or organised sports requiring significant financial investment, are less available to teenagers from lower-income families.

In India, where socioeconomic disparities are also pronounced, the types of play vary significantly between urban and rural teenagers. In rural areas, teenagers often engage in traditional games like *kabaddi or gilli-danda*, which require minimal resources but are rich in social interaction and physical engagement. Urban teenagers, especially those from middle- or upper-class backgrounds, are more likely to participate in digital play, including online gaming and social media, reflecting, again, the global influence of technology and the barriers to participation for those from a lower-income background. Globalisation has had a significant impact on what play looks like for adolescents, and teenagers around the world, regardless of cultural background, are increasingly engaging in play such as video gaming, social media, and online sports. In South Korea, video gaming is not only a popular form of play but also a competitive sport. The country is known for its vibrant eSports culture, where teenagers engage in multiplayer online games. Teenagers in South Korea often spend significant amounts of time in *PC bangs* (internet cafes), where they can play games with friends. While gaming serves as a social and competitive outlet, it has also raised concerns about gaming addiction and mental health, prompting the government to implement restrictions on gaming hours for minors.

We see differences in cultural attitudes to play when we look more closely at education systems. As mentioned earlier in the chapter, in Finland there is a strong cultural emphasis on the importance of play and relaxation for teenagers. Finnish schools promote a balanced approach to education, and frequent breaks and minimal homework allow students time for play and creative activities. In comparison, China puts a strong emphasis on academic achievement and the pressure to succeed in the *Gaokao* (college entrance exam). As a result, teenagers often spend the majority of their time studying or participating in structured activities that enhance their academic profiles. While play is still present, particularly in the form of digital gaming or physical exercise, it is often seen as a luxury rather than a necessity. What we see across the globe are the changing types of play that young people engage in and the pressures that come from target-driven societies. However, as we have explored throughout this book, play brings positive results across all areas of the teenagers' growth and development.

The role of cultural norms in shaping adolescent play

Cultural values significantly influence how teenagers engage in play, particularly in terms of which activities are considered appropriate or beneficial. In some societies, play is closely tied to family, community, or collective traditions, whereas in others, it may be more individualised or connected to personal development and success. For example, in collectivist cultures such as those found in many parts of East Asia, play during adolescence often involves shared responsibilities, intergenerational storytelling, or community-based arts and rituals, reflecting values of harmony, duty, and respect for elders (Chao & Tseng, 2002). In contrast, in more individualistic cultures, such as the UK or the US, teenage play is frequently positioned within frameworks of self-expression, competition, or goal-oriented achievement.

These differing cultural orientations shape not only what play looks like but also how it is valued and supported by adults. In some settings, particularly where academic success is heavily prioritised, adolescent play may be restricted or viewed as a distraction rather than a developmental right. Research by Goncu, Mistry, and Mosier (2000) highlights that adolescents' play preferences and freedoms are closely tied to culturally constructed expectations about maturity, productivity, and social roles. This can lead to unequal opportunities for play, with marginalised young people, such as girls, working-class teens, or migrants, often experiencing reduced access to playful spaces or being subject to adult surveillance and moral judgement. Understanding the cultural lens through which play is filtered is therefore essential when designing inclusive environments. Recognising and valuing culturally diverse forms of adolescent play not only affirm identity but also enable more authentic, context-sensitive approaches to youth work and education.

Exploring play for adolescents in tribal cultures

Play has been an essential element of human societies for millennia, acting as a vehicle for learning, socialisation, and cultural transmission. In tribal cultures around the world, play takes on a unique significance, especially for teenagers transitioning from childhood to adulthood. Unlike in more industrialised societies, where play might be compartmentalised into social periods of the day, tribal cultures often embed play deeply into everyday life, combining it with cultural traditions, survival skills, and social cohesion.

In many tribal cultures, play for teenagers serves as an important medium for passing down cultural knowledge, values, and traditions from one generation to the next. This is particularly true in cultures that rely on oral traditions and experiential learning rather than formal schooling. Play is often integrated with storytelling, music, dance, and other traditional practices that embody a tribe's history, mythology, and worldview.

Western societies have much to learn from these culturally embedded approaches to adolescent play. We have explored how in many industrialised contexts, play is increasingly marginalised, treated as a distraction from academic achievement, or confined to specific, time-bound slots. By contrast, tribal cultures demonstrate how play can be interwoven with identity, community, and intergenerational learning. These models remind us that play is not separate from learning or development but integral to them. Incorporating more holistic, culturally relevant, and community-led forms of play into Western settings could help reconnect adolescents with their heritage, build collective resilience, and reframe play as a lifelong human need rather than a childhood phase to be outgrown.

Play as a cultural transmission

In the San people of southern Africa, teenagers participate in traditional games that simulate hunting, gathering, and survival techniques. These activities are not merely for entertainment but are designed to teach important life skills, such as tracking animals, using tools, and understanding the natural environment. The San use mock hunts and tracking games to familiarise adolescents with the skills necessary for living and thriving in the Kalahari Desert. These activities also emphasise community values such as cooperation, patience, and respect for the natural world.

Similarly, in Australian Aboriginal cultures, play for teenagers often revolves around storytelling and Dreamtime narratives, which explain the creation of the world and the cultural laws that govern it. Adolescents may engage in role-playing games that reenact these mythological stories, helping them internalise the spiritual beliefs, social norms, and responsibilities that are seen as important for guiding them as adults. The use of games and play in this context serves as a rite of passage, allowing young people to actively participate in the perpetuation of their culture.

Together, these examples illustrate that play is not a trivial pastime but a profound medium through which cultural identities are shaped and sustained. For many indigenous communities, adolescent play is a serious form of cultural work: one that preserves ancestral knowledge, affirms group identity, and prepares young people for the moral and practical demands of adult life. This challenges Western notions of play as idle or optional, offering instead a vision of play as essential to the continuity and vitality of a community's way of being.

Play as preparation for adult roles

In many tribal cultures, play for teenagers not only is about fun or leisure but also serves as preparation for adult responsibilities. Play often mimics adult tasks and challenges, allowing teenagers to practice essential skills in a safe and supportive environment before they are expected to perform them in real life. This type of play is particularly important in subsistence-based societies, where survival depends on mastery of skills such as hunting, farming, or herding. (We will explore gender roles shortly.)

In the Inuit communities of the Arctic, play often involves activities that prepare teenagers for the harsh realities of their environment. Traditional Inuit games, such as *qilaut* (drum dancing) and *ajagaq* (a form of hunting game with a bone and string), help adolescents develop physical strength, hand-eye coordination, and endurance, which are crucial for hunting and navigating the Arctic terrain. These games also reinforce the cultural importance of resilience and adaptability, values that are essential for survival in such a challenging environment.

For the Yanomami people of the Amazon rainforest, play is a way for teenagers to prepare for the communal responsibilities they will take on as adults. Adolescent boys often engage in mock raids and wrestling matches that simulate the physical and strategic demands of adult life in a warrior society. These playful contests also serve as outlets for expressing and resolving conflicts, helping young people learn the importance of cooperation and negotiation within the tribe.

In Mongolian nomadic culture, teenage boys participate in horseback games like *shagai* (a game using the bones of sheep) and wrestling competitions that reflect the skills needed for herding and protecting livestock, the foundation of Mongolian nomadic life. Play in this context teaches not only physical prowess but also the deep connection to animals and the land that is central to Mongolian identity.

Gender roles and play

In many tribal cultures, the play activities of teenagers are strongly influenced by gender roles. Boys and girls are often expected to engage in different types of play that prepare them for the specific responsibilities they will assume in adulthood. However, these distinctions are not always rigid, and in some cases, play allows teenagers to explore and challenge traditional gender roles.

In Samoan culture, for instance, gendered play is prominent but flexible. Teenage boys engage in activities such as *fa'ataupati* (a form of traditional slap dancing) and mock fishing expeditions, preparing them for their roles as providers and protectors. Girls, on the other hand, participate in activities like weaving, cooking, and traditional dances, which prepare them for roles in maintaining the household and preserving cultural practices. However, Samoan society also allows for fluidity in these roles, and teenagers of either gender may participate in communal games or group activities that emphasise social cohesion and collective identity.

In the Himba people of Namibia, teenage girls often participate in play that mirrors the tasks of adult women, such as caring for younger siblings or preparing food. Boys, in contrast, engage in activities that develop their skills in herding and animal husbandry. Despite these gender distinctions, play for both boys and girls serves the dual purpose of skill acquisition and social integration, ensuring that all members of the community understand their roles and responsibilities within the tribe.

I would like you to recognise that highlighting gendered patterns of play in tribal cultures is not me endorsing rigid gender roles but an acknowledgment of how play reflects and responds to cultural values. From a Western feminist perspective, such examples might initially appear to reinforce traditional binaries; however, many of these practices involve far more nuance and flexibility than often assumed. Play in these contexts can offer teenagers the opportunity not only to acquire culturally relevant skills but also to explore identity and question societal expectations in a safe and symbolic space. As research in Western contexts also shows, when young people engage in role play, storytelling, or imitation, they often experiment with power dynamics, empathy, and identity beyond conventional roles (Renold, 2006). Rather than viewing gendered play solely through a restrictive lens, these cultural examples invite a broader understanding of play as a medium for learning, negotiation, and, in some cases, subtle resistance.

Rites of passage and the role of play

Play is deeply embedded in the life of tribal adolescents. While the specific forms of play vary across cultures, the purpose remains the same: to help teenagers navigate the complex transition from childhood to adulthood and integrate into the social and cultural fabric of their communities. As global influences and modernisation continue to impact tribal societies, the role of play in these cultures may evolve, but its fundamental importance as a tool for learning and cultural continuity is likely to endure. Understanding the role of play in tribal cultures provides valuable insights into the ways in which human societies, past and present, have used play to educate, socialise, and prepare young people for the challenges and opportunities of adult life. As a researcher who has explored intergenerational learning, I find that appreciation for our heritage and the generations that have come before us is a key area of focus. We have a lot to learn from looking outside of an individualistic lens.

For many tribal cultures, adolescence is marked by formal rites of passage that signify the transition from childhood to adulthood. Play is often incorporated into these rites, serving as a form of preparation, testing, or symbolic representation of the challenges and responsibilities that come with adulthood. In the Suri people of Ethiopia, adolescent boys undergo a rite of passage called *donga*, a ritualised stick-fighting competition. This form of play is both a test of physical strength and endurance and a means of demonstrating readiness for adult responsibilities. While the fights are serious and can result in injury, they are also seen as a form of play in which young men can compete for honour and status within the community. Through this ritualised form of play, Suri teenagers explore the values of courage, discipline, and respect. But how might this play look in Western society, and is rough-and-tumble play something that young people want to experience? I have found myself observing this type of play unintentionally as I collect my own teens from school over the past few weeks. As I sit waiting for my children to leave for the day (I am not sure why my children always seem to be the last ones out!), I park up next to a grassed area, close to the bus stop. The young males physically tumble over each other, trying to whip the legs out from the other. As I start to wonder if intervention is needed (my children would love to leave school and observe me out of the car pulling their friends apart!), I see the teens reaching out a hand to help one another up and doubling over with laughter. There is no bullying or nastiness in what they are doing. They are playing and letting off steam in a way that is effective for them, knowing the boundaries, and respecting one another's playful cues.

Reflection

When we truly observe young people, across cultures, communities, and contexts, we see that their play is rich with meaning, even when it appears chaotic, quiet, or nonconforming to adult expectations. From communal storytelling in Aboriginal cultures to rough-and-tumble play outside school gates, true play persists because it speaks to something fundamental: the need to connect, explore, test boundaries, and make sense of the world on one's own terms. In Western education systems, we are often so focused on outcomes, measurements, and performance that we overlook what play can teach us. True play cannot be prescribed or assessed, yet it is where some of the most powerful learning happens. As adults, we need to unlearn the idea that play must always serve a visible, measurable purpose. True play resists that framing. It is expansive, relational, and often beautifully unpredictable. What we can learn from observing true play in adolescent spaces is that trust matters. When we trust young people with time, space, and autonomy, they respond by showing us what they need, what they value, and who they are becoming.

References

Brown, S. (2009) *Play: How It Shapes the Brain, Opens the Imagination, and Invigorates the Soul*. New York: Avery.

Chao, R.K. and Tseng, V. (2002) 'Parenting of Asians', in M.H. Bornstein (ed.) *Handbook of Parenting*, Vol. 4. Mahwah, NJ: Lawrence Erlbaum Associates, pp. 59–93.

Fredricks, J.A. and Simpkins, S.D. (2012) 'Promoting positive youth development through organized after-school activities: Taking a closer look at participation of ethnic minority youth', *Child Development Perspectives*, 6(3), pp. 280–287.

Goncu, A., Mistry, J. and Mosier, C. (2000) 'Cultural variations in the play of toddlers', *International Journal of Behavioral Development*, 24(3), pp. 321–329.

Gray, P. (2013) *Free to Learn: Why Unleashing the Instinct to Play Will Make Our Children Happier, More Self-Reliant, and Better Students for Life*. New York: Basic Books.

Hughes, B. (2001) *Evolutionary Playwork and Reflective Analytic Practice*. London: Routledge.

Lester, S. and Russell, W. (2008) *Play for a Change: Play, Policy and Practice: A Review of Contemporary Perspectives*. London: Play England.

Renold, E. (2006) '"They won't let us play... unless you're going out with one of them": Girls, boys and Butler's "heterosexual matrix" in the primary years', *British Journal of Sociology of Education*, 27(4), pp. 489–509.

Chapter 14

Play at breaktimes

During a visit to universities and colleges in China, I spent a free afternoon with colleagues taking a walk in a park. The weather was glorious, and it was lovely to see people fully utilising the space and making the most of downtime. The park was much bigger than I was used to and had a great variety of activities that visitors could partake in. This included an allotment-style sustainability garden, used by community groups and schools, to rowing boats on the lake, to a huge theme park-style section with several rollercoasters and merry-go-rounds. By the time we found the theme park, we realised we had walked for miles, and it was much more advanced than the usual recreational space that we were used to. For someone who has spent some years reviewing intergenerational learning, I thought it was wonderful to see how families seemed to be valuing the time to bring all generations together during their downtime. Although the park was much bigger and hosted many different recreational areas, I smiled as I watched younger children fascinated by the autumnal leaves, making them crunch under their feet and exploring their texture and patterns. The rollercoaster will never beat the pleasure of jumping through leaves!

It was this observation that made me reflect on our own public parks that we have in the UK. I find the designs frequently frustrating as we segregate areas for different age groups and limit spaces dependent on activity. An example of this is the traditional climbing frames and swings. If we see teenagers using the swings, what is our initial reaction? Many readers here will be play advocates, but I know that this scene may bring annoyance, worry, or fear. For most adolescents who sit on the swing seat and kick their legs up in the air, all they are seeking is some fun. It is not only systems that delete play out of the teenage years but also societal views on how young people should conform. Not only should teenagers be seeking out play, but we also need to remember, as a society, that there are limited spaces tailored to this stage of life – so where else have they got to go during their social breaks?

In countries such as Sweden, schools often integrate outdoor play and physical activity into the curriculum through *Friluftsliv*, a Norwegian concept that encourages outdoor education and connection with nature. The philosophy of *Friluftsliv* is that humans participate in a simple life, alongside nature, minimising the impact on the natural world. In studies undertaken by Dahlgren and Szczepanski (2007), they found that students who participated in regular outdoor play displayed stronger focus, their academic performance improved, and there was increased motivation to learn. This aligns with research from across Europe that shows physical activity improves not only physical health but also adolescents' cognitive outcomes.

Humans are not made to sit at desks for six hours, and we are increasingly seeing not just adults but teenagers *and* children spending all their time indoors, sitting in a similar position. A report by Clip 'n Climb (2020) found that, on an average weekend, children in the US and Germany spend over 20 hours indoors as opposed to children in the UK and Japan, who spend between 15.5 and 16.5 hours indoors. However, the report provides us with a challenge as it also found that teenagers voiced that they wanted to spend their free time indoors rather than spending time outside. With technology being a key social activity for young people, and limited public places in the community for young people to spend their free time in, policymakers and urban designers need to reflect on how they develop communities that adolescents feel secure and happy in. The evidence on the benefits of being outdoors far outweighs those that we see on gaming and social network activity. This is not to dismiss utilising digital technologies, and I will indeed discuss them in this chapter; however, when planning for play breaks, we need to prioritise the connection with the natural world to provide opportunities that tackle a generational group experiencing play deprivation.

Creating spaces for play in the setting grounds

Schools, colleges, and other educational settings should provide areas where teenagers feel safe and comfortable engaging in play. This might include open areas for physical activities, indoor spaces for quieter or creative play, and spaces where digital gaming can be enjoyed, as appropriate. As we review the layout of our educational settings, we see more educators and classes moving out of the classroom and into other areas of the building and playground to learn. These spaces can also be utilised for breaktimes, and play areas can help to minimise negative disruptions that can be found when teenagers get bored. I have recently observed how a ping-pong table in the corridor has re-established a space that was previously loitered in to one where people who do not generally talk to one another now come together as a team, smiling, laughing, and encouraging their peers whilst bringing a lot of joy to those who walk past. Laughter and happiness are contagious; the more we observe it, the happier we feel.

The teenage playground is often very similar in layout to the ones found in primary schools but without the climbing frames and loose equipment. Sports can frequently still be seen, with someone bringing in a ball to kick about or play hoop with. This suits those who enjoy sports, but what about those that do not? If you were to put some chalks and bottles of bubbles out in the playground, I can almost guarantee that once teenagers notice them, laughter and togetherness will come from engaging with the play cue. Breaktimes are for fun, and we need to remind young people that life does not need to be serious all the time.

Play can be the most productive way to minimise the negative behaviours often associated with the teenage years. If you have a problem with graffiti in your school, why not call for a group to design a graffiti mural that represents your settings values? If you have older teens disengaged, provide them with the opportunity to teach younger peers how to play a game of cards or how to use sound and rhythm on apps to mix tracks together. I am not saying we should be rewarding negative behaviours, but we should be engaging young people to minimise the causes of disruptive activities. Incorporating play can prevent boredom and focus attention on activities that boost positive endorphins.

Facilitating peer-led play

Teenagers often prefer autonomy and may resist adult-led activities. Settings can encourage peer leadership by allowing students to organise and lead games or activities, promoting leadership skills, and giving them a sense of ownership over their breaktime. Teenagers will spend lengthy periods of the day following the rules set by adults. If we were to tell a group of adolescents to go outside and play, I can feel the eyeroll that would come our way in response. If we are truly committed to play, it is a positive starting point to get the teens on board and for them to take ownership of the activities and spaces. Teenagers will also speak differently to one another when adults are out of the way and can enjoy being themselves without worrying about an adult's expectations of how they interact. Of course, if individuals are speaking negatively to one another, adult intervention is a must, but I focus here on the relaxed discussions that come amongst friends in their downtime. A school might have different student committees such as one that focuses on mental health, entrepreneurship, or a school council. Why not introduce one that focuses on play. You might be pleasantly surprised with the fun activities that the committee comes up with, and teamwork leads to cohesiveness and builds a stronger community.

Balancing structure and freedom

While some adolescents may enjoy structured play (like organised sports), others may prefer unstructured, spontaneous play. Settings should balance both by offering opportunities for free play alongside optional, organised activities. In a study from Mahoney, Cairns, and Farmer (2003), teenagers who engage in extracurricular and recreational activities experience lower levels of emotional distress and higher levels of wellbeing. Activities like basketball, tag, or other physical games during breaktime provide an outlet for excess energy and emotional release, an important release to place breaks in between timetabled lessons: but what outlet is there for those not engaging with the breaktime sports events?

Informal games, such as card games or chess, challenge teenagers to use logic and planning skills. During breaktime, teenagers can engage in games that require cognitive engagement without the pressure of academic performance, which can reinforce classroom learning in a relaxed environment. Worry and high levels of stress have a negative impact on not just our emotional but also our physical health. We need to consider the teenager who works through their breaks and how we encourage them to switch off and participate in something fun, alongside the individual who quietly worries independently, dissociated from the group. In Chapter 7, we explore the importance of role modelling play, and this is a key area where we can look after ourselves, alongside supporting the teenagers we work with. Take your break; do something fun with the other educators alongside the young people. Having a period of restful play and fun will make you more productive and encourage the young people to take your lead and engage in their own peer activities.

Promoting inclusivity

Adolescence is a time when social cliques can form, leading to feelings of exclusion for some students. Settings should emphasise inclusive play, offering activities that appeal to diverse interests and ensuring that no student feels left out. Consider how you incorporate play that reflects the students' own childhood experiences and is accessible for everybody to participate in. Young people want to fit in. They do not want to look silly or to stand out from their peers. Play spaces must feel safe and open for all involved. Boundaries do need to be in place to ensure this emotional security and to ensure that individuals within the group are not singled out for any negative reason. Think about what language is acceptable and how it must be used respectfully. Reflecting on the values of your group is important to build a sense of belonging and to ensure that people are respectful in their interactions. Using anonymous surveys can help to build play spaces that are valued by the group and ensure that the vision for play is built on the interests and ideas of those engaging in it. Sturrock and Else (2005) stress that adults should observe, interpret, and sensitively respond to support play without dominating or stifling it. Our responsibility, as facilitators, is to ensure that we reflect as play evolves to ensure that all can access and have their voice heard.

Mental health issues such as anxiety and depression often surface during adolescence, as discussed in Chapter 3. Play during breaktime can serve as a buffer against these challenges by promoting social inclusion and reducing feelings of loneliness. Research by Gilman, Huebner, and Laughlin (2000) suggests that recreational activities during school hours can enhance adolescents' self-esteem and mood, helping them cope with the pressures of academic life and peer relationships. By investing in a variety of different play types, we can ensure that there is fair access to play, with participation aligned with the teenagers' interests.

Challenges and considerations

While incorporating play into breaktimes for teenagers offers many benefits, there are challenges that schools need to consider in order to maximise its positive impact.

Peer pressure and social awareness: As we have just explored, adolescence is a period when peer dynamics and social hierarchies are strongly felt. Owing to fear of judgement, teenagers may feel reluctant to participate in playful activities or engage with activities in which their peer group is not interested. If the playground has a strong emphasis on play through sports, those who are not skilled at the activity may shy away from the activity, while others may feel excluded from group games dominated by cliques or more popular peers. Some sports are sometimes perceived as gendered and not open to all. To join a group, where you feel you do not fit, impacts further on social anxiety and can prevent some teenagers from experiencing the benefits of breaktime play. Settings can promote inclusive environments by understanding the playground dynamics. Staff can facilitate activities that emphasise collaboration rather than competition, such as cooperative games or creative projects that don't focus on winning.

Consideration should be given as to whether sports activities are accessible only for those accessing training or to one gender. Challenging assumptions and using role models that reflect the students can have a very positive impact on engagement. It is important for settings to offer a wide range of activities, including arts, sports, and intellectual games, so that diverse interests and abilities can be catered for and so the play is fun for all. Peer mentorship programmes or *play leaders* can also encourage more students to get involved by reducing social barriers and developing a more supportive atmosphere.

Physical environment and resources: Not all settings have the facilities or resources to provide a diverse range of playful activities during breaktime. Limited outdoor space, lack of equipment, or even the weather can restrict opportunities for active play and to get outdoors. Additionally, settings with fewer financial resources may struggle to offer materials such as art supplies or board games. Settings can adopt a resourceful approach to maximise the use of available space and resources. Multi-purpose equipment like balls, packs of playing cards, or chalk can be used for a variety of games and activities. For a recent 'Outdoor Classroom Day', a national event to promote outdoor learning, I provided teenagers with some packs of chalks at breaktime. These could be collected at the front door, and students were given permission to use them wherever they wanted to in the college outdoor space. It was a great success, with a morning full of connection and laughter. Students wrote positive messages, drew out hopscotch to play on, and we saw some real artistic skills come from the students. Before we try these activities, we might think students this age have outgrown them. But when we provide them with the resources, we're often pleasantly surprised. Using indoor spaces or classrooms to play low-cost board games and puzzles can provide a space for teenagers to find some peace during breaks. Over my years of education, I have learnt many new card games by joining students on breaks and presenting a pack of cards on the table.

Settings may also wish to partner with local sports clubs or community organisations to share facilities. Contacting local businesses to sponsor equipment or offer volunteers to lead breaktime activities can also be a way to extend play opportunities for the young people in your organisation.

Safety and supervision: Ensuring safety during breaktime play is a key concern for settings. Play can result in accidents, particularly during physical games or sports, and schools must be prepared to manage risk. This does not mean removing risk, as risk provides a valuable learning opportunity, but consideration does have to be given as to how play might look in our environments. The balance between autonomy in play and providing appropriate supervision can be challenging, especially when this is often the time when we as educators need a much-deserved break ourselves! Over-supervision can also inhibit the free, exploratory nature of play, so consideration needs to be given as to what your play vision is for your setting and how the adult's role looks during this period of the day. Settings can implement supervision strategies that ensure safety without undermining students' independence, and those supervising breaktimes can be trained to observe from a distance, intervening only when necessary.

Maybe in your school's culture, breaktimes are not for playful interactions, so play is not something you have observed in your spaces. But with encouragement, educators or support workers can be facilitators of activities such as sports or game stations and act as role models and encouragers. Once the culture has shifted to one in which these activities are a normalised part of the breaktimes, adults will be able to step back and trust in students to use the resources appropriately, managing risk independently as a peer group. Having designated spaces for different activities, such as a games room or a particular sports pitch that can be used, not only minimises risk but provides students with an understanding that they can use the space in an engaged way.

Time restraints and academic pressures: In some educational settings, especially in highly competitive academic environments, the time allocated for breaktime may be limited due to a focus on maximising the educational hours within the day. In such cases, students may not have enough time to fully engage in meaningful play, and this can impact their ability to de-stress and socialise. Academic pressures may also lead students to choose to spend their breaktime studying or completing homework rather than playing. I can appreciate the focus, but I must stress the importance of switching off and gaining downtime throughout the day. We all need it, whether that be student, educator, or support worker. By prioritising and role modelling a balanced approach, we show students that we recognise the importance of taking time out of the day to enjoy the social aspect of the settings environment, in turn, focusing on the teenagers' holistic development. Educators can work to shift the cultural narrative by promoting the benefits of play as essential for cognitive and emotional health rather than framing it as time away from academic productivity. Have you got a box of dominoes in your staff room? Some books of crosswords? Or some print-outs of lunchtime riddles that could go into a box at the end of break for a token prize? Role-modelling play can help everyone see its benefits and value why it is needed for the young people you work with.

The importance of playful break periods

Tomporowski et al. (2008) conducted research demonstrating that students who engage in regular physical play exhibit better concentration and self-regulation in academic tasks. This supports the idea that play is not a distraction from learning but rather a vital component of cognitive development. Play should be not just integrated into lessons but embedded in a meaningful way during break periods. Asian education systems, particularly in Singapore, have embraced this understanding, and schools promote a balance between academic rigour and physical education to optimise learning outcomes. These findings further support the need for integration of physical play into secondary school curricula, particularly in competitive academic environments such as South Korea and China, where students could benefit from improved focus and cognitive performance after engaging in physical activity.

With the increasing use of technology and sedentary lifestyles among teenagers, breaktime play serves as a critical moment to engage in physical activity. Active play reduces the risk of obesity, improves cardiovascular health, and boosts overall fitness levels. By encouraging healthy choices and habits in the teenage years, we are establishing routines that they will carry forward with them into adult life. The UK Chief Medical Officers recommend that adolescents engage in at least 60 minutes of moderate to vigorous physical activity daily, and breaktimes offer a key opportunity to contribute to this target. Active games and sports during these times promote lifelong habits of physical health and wellbeing (Department of Health and Social Care, 2019). Play habits can be instrumental not just for welling and academic success but for health as well.

References

Clip 'n Climb (2020) *Youth Activity Patterns: Indoor vs Outdoor Play in Global Cities*. Available at: https://clipnclimb.com (Accessed: 14 June 2025).

Dahlgren, L.O. and Szczepanski, A. (2007) *Outdoor Education – Literary Education and Sensory Experience: An Empirical Study of Outdoor Education in Sweden*. Linköping: Linköping University.

Department of Health and Social Care (2019) *UK Chief Medical Officers' Physical Activity Guidelines*. Available at: https://www.gov.uk/government/publications/physical-activity-guidelines-uk-chief-medical-officers-report (Accessed: 14 June 2025).

Gilman, R., Huebner, E.S. and Laughlin, J.E. (2000) 'A first study of the multidimensional students' life satisfaction scale with adolescents', *Social Indicators Research*, 52(2), pp. 135–160.

Mahoney, J.L., Cairns, B.D. and Farmer, T.W. (2003) 'Promoting interpersonal competence and educational success through extracurricular activity participation', *Journal of Educational Psychology*, 95(2), pp. 409–418.

Sturrock, G. and Else, P. (2005) *The Play Cycle: Theory, Research and Application*. Sheffield: Common Threads Publications.

Tomporowski, P.D., Davis, C.L., Miller, P.H. and Naglieri, J.A. (2008) 'Exercise and children's intelligence, cognition, and academic achievement', *Educational Psychology Review*, 20(2), pp. 111–131.

Chapter 15

Play after school

During adolescence, play continues to serve as a powerful medium for social connection, identity exploration, and emotional resilience. In increasingly pressured school environments, opportunities for voluntary, interest-led play become essential for promoting wellbeing and supporting social development, and periods after school can be a beneficial time to implement play sessions. It can also be a good starting point to create a playful culture that will influence the rest of the school day.

We have seen how apparent it is throughout this book that play is essential in developing social competencies such as communication, cooperation, and conflict resolution, all of which are crucial for success in both academic and real-world scenarios. Zarrett et al. (2009) found that participation in team-based play activities, such as sports or group-based projects, positively impacts teenagers' social skills. This is particularly valuable in the competitive environments of countries where collaboration may not always be emphasised in traditional classroom settings. After-school clubs can be a great mechanism for ensuring that young people get access to playful activities that support these areas of development. Meaningful sessions can ensure that adolescents have full agency in this space and that experiences can reflect the interests of those in attendance.

Global approaches to extracurricular play

Around the world, schools are responding to the developmental needs of adolescents by embedding play in extracurricular life. Hong Kong has a strong tradition of extracurricular activities, and schools offer a wide range of clubs and societies where students can engage in playful learning experiences. For example, students may participate in drama clubs, debating teams, or science clubs, where they engage in playful exploration of topics that interest them. Schools also organise experiential learning opportunities such as trips and project-based learning, where students learn by engaging in hands-on, playful activities that develop critical thinking and problem-solving skills.

The role of extracurricular activities, such as Japan's Bukatsu (club activities), is a prime example of how play can support social development. By participating in team sports, drama clubs, and musical activities, students learn to collaborate towards common goals, developing leadership and interpersonal skills that are crucial both in school and later in professional life. Park and Kim (2016) found that these activities significantly contribute to the social development of students in South Korea, where the education system is slowly incorporating more play-based social learning into its curriculum to combat the negative effects of extreme academic pressure. Park and Kim's (2016) research on South Korea's education reforms, particularly the introduction of play-based learning, on student wellbeing and academic performance suggests that while the traditional academic structure in South Korea is highly competitive, the introduction of play-based activities, especially in extracurricular settings, has contributed to reducing student stress and improving overall wellbeing.

In Western contexts, particularly the US and parts of Europe, play is increasingly framed as innovation. 'Maker Spaces', creative, hands-on environments for building and experimenting, have grown popular in secondary schools. Peppler and Bender (2013) describe how these settings support autonomous learning and intrinsic motivation, enabling adolescents to become confident problem-solvers. The deep concentration and satisfaction that students often experience in such environments align with Csikszentmihalyi's (1990) notion of *flow* (as explored in Chapter 2), a state in which individuals are fully immersed in a meaningful challenge. Activities that support flow are not just enjoyable; they also promote self-efficacy and long-term engagement with learning.

Play in practice

Typical after-school activities might include sports programmes or dance groups, and these are great ways to engage young people with movement and play, but this will not suit all teens' interests and can even segregate those who do not enjoy competitive environments. So, what alternatives can we offer? Play leader sessions can be a great way for the school community to come together and embed a mentorship scheme between younger and older pupils. In these sessions, older students will facilitate the after-school sessions for younger peers, planning inclusive games and cooperative challenges. More than just a leadership exercise, the programme became a space for playful relationship-building, where students across year groups found common ground. It also provides an opening for older adolescents to engage in play. To extend this activity further, you could also partner with a primary school and run the sessions for younger children and build community links.

In a school in Helsinki, staff developed the *Creative Lab*, an informal media workshop held after school. Students worked in small teams to produce films, podcasts, and performances on themes they selected themselves. What set the Lab apart was its open-ended, exploratory ethos: students were not told what to create but rather given tools and encouragement to follow their curiosity. According to Hietala (2021), this resulted in greater engagement from students who typically struggled in traditional classroom settings, especially those with learning needs.

In a collaborative project between educators and artists in New York, a school created outdoor *urban playgrounds* as part of a local arts initiative. Students constructed installations, performed original scripts, and transformed the playground into a social and creative commons. As Danko and Greene (2020) note, this supported a sense of belonging and pride while embedding civic themes into playful spaces.

At a middle school in Pittsburgh, USA, *Lego Brick Clubs* became an inclusive and popular fixture of school life. Designed initially to support neurodivergent students, the club attracted wide participation. Pupils built story scenes, designed machines, and tackled building challenges in small groups. According to a report by Play Included (2023), the sessions significantly improved peer relationships, and students reported feeling calmer and more focused after participating. These Lego clubs exemplify the kind of structured, creative play that supports both social and emotional development in adolescence.

Although these activities are very different, play is woven throughout all the activities and draws on the experiences and interests of the young people participating.

Designing playful after-school activities

Reflecting on the examples of playful after-school activities, schools can implement after-school activities that prioritise student voice, support collaborative exploration, and make space for failure as part of the learning process. Game design clubs could be used to offer adolescents the opportunity to invent, test, and refine board or digital games, and students can attend workshops to create apps or games to support younger pupils with their literacy and numeracy skills whilst promoting their own knowledge in the process. Not only do these clubs promote strategic thinking and design literacy, but they also reflect the social nature of adolescent play, requiring negotiation, feedback, and iteration.

You may consider introducing improvisation or pop-up theatre nights, which invite students to explore narrative, humour, and social issues in a low-pressure environment. For students less inclined to perform, backstage and production roles offer alternative paths for contribution. These activities often lead to unexpected collaborations, developing new friendships that cut across social cliques. More informal after-school clubs can include *Teach Me* clubs, where students take turns showing peers how to do something playful, whether that is a dance, a magic trick, or a football skill. These clubs showcase adolescents' diverse talents while supporting confidence and peer respect.

Meanwhile, robotics and LEGO storytelling clubs bring together logic and imagination, appealing to students' different interests.

Nature can be utilised, and I would encourage more clubs to take place outside following students' days in the classroom. Structured challenges such as scavenger hunts or creative tasks like natural sculpture-making offer physical movement and emotional release. When designed collaboratively with students, these activities often reflect themes they care about, such as sustainability, mental health, or community identity. With adolescents engaging with news through online, instant-access mechanisms, we can encourage conversations around what they are seeing and turn these into an activity that connects them with the world around them in a positive manner. These activities, when supported by trusting relationships and safe environments, invite the flow experience that underpins intrinsic motivation. As Bronfenbrenner (1979) suggests, these moments of deep engagement are not incidental. They are signs that the young person is thriving in an environment that recognises and nurtures their potential.

Overcoming barriers to implementation

Despite the compelling benefits, schools may face significant barriers when introducing or sustaining playful after-school activities. Limited funding, staff capacity, and timetable constraints are common challenges, as is the perception that play is less valuable than academic pursuits. In some settings, the culture of performativity, driven by exam results and inspection frameworks, can discourage risk-taking or non-assessed learning. Educators may also lack confidence in facilitating open-ended, student-led sessions.

Overcoming these barriers requires a whole-school commitment to valuing play as part of adolescent development. Crucially, support from senior leadership teams and governing bodies can legitimise and protect time and resources for play-based initiatives. Aligning activities with existing school priorities, such as wellbeing, inclusion, or leadership development, can also help embed them into the school culture. Drawing on the unique identity and values of each setting is vital: clubs that reflect local culture, community interests, or school ethos are more likely to thrive. There may also be a need for investment into professional development for staff, especially in areas like facilitation, co-creation, and inclusive practice. Having play on the professional development plan for the full staff team can build the confidence and skills needed to sustain a vibrant, playful after-school culture.

References

Bronfenbrenner, U. (1979) *The Ecology of Human Development: Experiments by Nature and Design.* Cambridge, MA: Harvard University Press.
Csikszentmihalyi, M. (1990) *Flow: The Psychology of Optimal Experience.* New York: Harper & Row.

Danko, M. and Greene, S. (2020) 'Playful public space: Youth-led design in urban environments', *Youth and Environments*, 30(1), pp. 22–40.

Hietala, A. (2021) 'Creative labs and inclusion: Enhancing engagement through media literacy', *Nordic Journal of Digital Literacy*, 16(3), pp. 145–162.

Park, S. and Kim, Y. (2016) 'Play-based learning reforms in South Korea: Addressing academic pressure through extracurricular programmes', *Asian Education Review*, 12(2), pp. 109–126.

Peppler, K. and Bender, S. (2013) 'Maker movement spreads innovation one project at a time', *Phi Delta Kappan*, 95(3), pp. 22–27.

Play Included (2023) *Lego® Based Therapy in Schools: Impact and Inclusion Report*. Available at: https://www.playincluded.com (Accessed: 14 June 2025).

Zarrett, N., Fay, K., Li, Y., Carrano, J., Phelps, E. and Lerner, R.M. (2009) 'More than child's play: Variable- and pattern-centered approaches for examining effects of sports participation on youth development', *Developmental Psychology*, 45(2), pp. 368–382.

Chapter 16

Developing a lifetime commitment to play

What is the best concert you have ever been to? I know mine: Tina Turner at Wembley on her final world tour. I had grown up with her energy catapulting through the screen, and *Proud Mary* is still a sure-fire tune to get my friends and I up on the dance floor. Tina Turner was a born performer, her commitment to putting on the best performance for her fans evident.

One of the reasons why this was my favourite concert was that it showed me what a legend Tina was. She covered every inch of the stage, playing with movements and sound, performing moves that most of us would not be able to comprehend. As she left the main stage, I was positioned to still see her, and those off-stage wrapped her tightly with a silver blanket. Her performance required the utmost care after completion. In her autobiography years later, Turner shared how those high-energy performances brought her deep joy. They were not just routines but acts of expression, bursting with playful interaction, between her and the music, her and the crowd, and even between her and herself. This idea, that playfulness can transcend childhood and become a way of being, is central to developing a lifetime commitment to play.

Cultivating lifelong playfulness from adolescence into adulthood

Throughout this book, we have seen that although play is often positioned as the territory of childhood, something we are expected to grow out of, it is, in-fact, rather something we should grow with. A growing body of research from psychology, wellbeing science, and neuroscience makes this apparent: we do not stop needing play as we age. In fact, playfulness is increasingly recognised as a protective factor for mental health and emotional resilience across the lifespan. Research from Barnett (2011) states that adults who maintain a playful disposition report higher levels of life satisfaction, lower stress, and greater capacity for flexible thinking. Similarly, Proyer et al. (2020) found that adult playfulness is associated with positive emotional traits such as cheerfulness, humour, and the ability to cope with difficult emotions. Playfulness contributes to social connectedness, protects against depressive symptoms, and

DOI: 10.4324/9781003562368-17

supports adaptive coping strategies in the face of life stressors (Proyer, 2017; Pang & Proyer, 2018). These findings position play not as frivolous but as a core element of psychological wellbeing and lifelong learning.

Different types of play to cultivate a lifetime commitment to playfulness

Imaginative play is the internal theatre of possibility. It allows us to simulate futures, rework the past, and escape the constraints of the present. While often associated with children dressing up or creating fantasy worlds, imagination is no less critical in adulthood. In fact, it may become even more necessary as life grows more structured and routine-bound. As adults, we use imaginative play in everyday ways, planning holidays we might never take, rehearsing conversations in our heads, visualising goals, or even engaging in daydreams that lighten a difficult day. Psychologist Ruth Richards (2007) argues that imagination is not a luxury but a survival skill: it helps us reframe experiences, tolerate ambiguity, and find solutions beyond the obvious. Through imaginative play, we remain adaptable and expansive rather than fixed or cynical. Imaginative play keeps the mind flexible and the spirit alive. It gives us permission to step out of the ordinary and into what could be. When we encourage teenagers to retain this inner resource, not as something childish but as something powerful, we are investing in their ability to navigate life's uncertainties with creativity and vision.

In adolescence, social play serves as a testing ground for relationships. Banter, roleplay, group games, and performative humour allow young people to explore group dynamics, negotiate boundaries, and experiment with identity. If they are encouraged, this kind of playful relating teaches young people how to laugh at themselves, how to defuse tension, and how to build intimacy through shared happiness. These are skills we carry into romantic partnerships, friendships, parenting, and workplace relationships. However, in adulthood, the space for social play is often squeezed out. Conversations become transactional, time becomes rationed, and emotional expression becomes guarded. Yet research shows that adults who continue to engage in social play, through humour, games, storytelling, or improvisation, report stronger relationships, lower loneliness, and greater life satisfaction (Proyer & Jehle, 2013). Moments of play with others allow us to co-create meaning, celebrate differences, and take off defensive armour. Social play does not require perfect timing or performance. It simply requires presence and the willingness to engage with others in a spirit of curiosity and care. By embedding social play in adolescence as a way of *relating* and not just entertaining, we support a model of connection that can last a lifetime.

Creative play, whether through art, music, writing, storytelling, or making, offers a profound way of staying connected to ourselves and the world around us. It invites imagination, curiosity, and experimentation. Importantly, creative play provides a space where there are no right answers and where failure becomes part of the process rather than something to be feared. These qualities make it a powerful source of psychological nourishment throughout life. In adolescence, creative play allows young people to explore identity and self-expression in flexible and often subversive ways. Zines, playlists, photography, memes, and fashion become mediums of communication and cultural commentary. But creative play does not have to be left behind with teenage journals or art class projects. When nurtured beyond adolescence, it evolves into practices that support mental health, purpose, and pleasure in adulthood. Engaging in creative play as an adult offers an antidote to the productivity-driven mindset that often dominates professional and domestic life. Whether it's journalling without purpose, painting for enjoyment, making music with friends, or crafting something by hand, creative acts make room for presence and emotional release. Research has shown that even ten minutes of creative activity a day can reduce stress, enhance positive emotions, and increase psychological resilience (Fancourt & Finn, 2019).

Physical play, such as sports, dance, walking, and movement-based activities, is a form of engagement that can accompany us through every stage of life. Its value goes far beyond physical health. Physical play reconnects us to our bodies, reduces mental fatigue, and provides a crucial release valve for stress. Ratey and Hagerman (2008) found that regular movement boosts brain function, elevates mood, and supports mental clarity, benefits that are just as important in middle age and later life as they are in adolescence. When we experience running, jumping, stretching, or dancing as liberating rather than labour, we are more likely to return to it in adulthood: not out of obligation but from desire. The most enduring forms of physical play are those infused with laughter, social connection, and self-expression: dancing in the kitchen, hiking with friends, joining a community sports team, or simply choosing to walk rather than drive. These acts root us in the moment and offer accessible ways to experience vitality, regardless of age.

Throughout this book, we have seen a vast variety of play strategies. These are beneficial not just to the young people we work with but also to you. If you have fallen out of play or find it lost from your routine, bring it back. Dance like no one is watching and kick your shoes off to run across the grass.

Strategies for making a lifetime commitment to play

Embracing a playful mindset: One of the most powerful strategies for developing a lifelong commitment to play is cultivating a playful mindset. This mindset shifts an individual's perspective to approach life's tasks and challenges with curiosity, exploration, and flexibility rather than rigidity or stress. A playful mindset involves seeing potential for enjoyment and creative thinking in routine activities as well as being open to spontaneous opportunities for fun. A person with a playful outlook views challenges as puzzles to solve rather than obstacles to overcome, making even difficult tasks more engaging. Adults who adopt a playful mindset experience less stress and greater creativity (Bateson & Martin, 2013). This can be fostered by incorporating humour, light-heartedness, and experimentation into everyday life. For example, instead of seeing work meetings as purely functional, you may wish to shift the approach and see these as an opportunity for creative problem-solving or brainstorming techniques to generate new ideas. By reframing experiences with a sense of play, individuals can find more joy in daily activities and maintain their connection to play across the lifespan.

Incorporating play into daily routines: Building play into daily routines is another useful strategy for sustaining playfulness throughout life. While play is often associated with leisure time, integrating small moments of play into everyday tasks can keep the habit alive. This could involve incorporating play into work tasks, such as using creative thinking techniques or gamifying challenges to make them more enjoyable. For example, setting small, fun challenges for completing tasks at work can break up the monotony and introduce a sense of achievement and joy. Physical activities, such as taking playful breaks during work hours, stretching, dancing, or engaging in short, interactive exercises, can also re-energise the body and mind. Studies suggest that brief periods of playful movement during the day can improve focus, reduce stress, and increase overall wellbeing (Rogers et al., 2019). Similarly, incorporating creative play, such as doodling, crafting, or playing an instrument during downtime, can enhance cognitive flexibility and emotional resilience.

Pursuing play-focused leisure activities: Deliberately choosing leisure activities that emphasise play is a key way to ensure that play remains a central part of life. Adults who maintain hobbies that involve play are more likely to continue engaging in playful activities into their later years. These hobbies can range from physically active pursuits, such as team sports, dancing, or hiking, to mentally engaging activities like board games, role-playing games, or puzzles. Social games, such as escape rooms or quiz nights, provide both intellectual stimulation and a sense of camaraderie, blending play with social connection. Importantly, play-focused leisure activities provide the opportunity for adults to experience fun without the pressure of productivity, allowing for relaxation and rejuvenation. When adults see play as a legitimate use of time, they create space in their schedules for fun, which in turn strengthens their commitment to playful activities over the long term (Kaufman & Gregoire, 2015). Encouraging participation in creative arts, such as theatre, music, or visual arts, continues to develop the playful mindset, as these activities engage the imagination and allow for self-expression.

Promoting play in social relationships: Play is often a social activity, and relationships play a critical role in sustaining a lifelong commitment to play. Surrounding oneself with people who value and engage in play can help normalise playful behaviour for adults and create more opportunities for playful interactions. For example, playful friendships often involve shared jokes, games, and creative activities that reinforce bonds and promote joy. In intimate relationships, playfulness has been shown to increase satisfaction and emotional connection (Proyer, 2014), helping to maintain a sense of fun even in serious partnerships. Building a social network that supports play might involve joining community groups or clubs that focus on playful activities, such as sports leagues, hobby clubs, or creative workshops. These social contexts provide consistent opportunities for playful engagement and allow individuals to connect with others who share a commitment to maintaining playfulness.

Lifelong learning and play: Lifelong learning and play are closely linked, as both require curiosity, openness to new experiences, and creative thinking. Engaging in learning opportunities, whether formal or informal, can be a playful pursuit when approached with the right mindset. Taking on new challenges, learning new skills, and exploring unfamiliar topics are all playful acts of intellectual engagement. For instance, learning a new language, taking up a musical instrument, or mastering a craft can be seen as playful ways to stimulate the mind and challenge oneself. Research shows that adults who maintain an attitude of curiosity and embrace opportunities for learning are more likely to experience cognitive benefits and emotional wellbeing (Seligman, 2011). By viewing learning as a form of play, individuals can stay intellectually active and maintain a sense of wonder throughout life. This approach not only enhances cognitive flexibility but also builds a positive relationship with challenge, making play a key component of lifelong learning.

Overcoming barriers to committing to play

Maintaining a lifelong commitment to play requires overcoming significant barriers, such as societal expectations, time constraints, and personal attitudes that devalue play in adulthood. Overcoming this mindset involves recognising the benefits of play, not just for relaxation but also for cognitive development, emotional wellbeing, and social connection. Strategies for overcoming these barriers include setting clear boundaries between work and leisure time, so that play is prioritised as an essential activity. Additionally, adults can practice integrating play into their responsibilities, such as turning daily routines or family time into playful experiences. This approach helps balance the demands of adulthood with the need for playful engagement, making play an integral part of life rather than something reserved for rare moments of leisure.

Technology and play

As we have seen throughout this book and, I am sure, also through your own experiences, technology has become an increasingly important tool for play, offering new avenues for engagement through video games, virtual reality, and online social interactions. Adults who embrace playful technology, such as gaming or digital art, can experience cognitive and social benefits. Multiplayer online games, for example, provide a platform for social interaction and strategic thinking, while virtual reality games offer immersive environments that encourage exploration and creativity (Granic et al., 2014).

However, it is important to balance technology use with physical and social play to ensure a well-rounded experience. Over-reliance on digital play can lead to sedentary behaviour or reduced face-to-face interactions, so integrating both traditional and technology-based forms of play can help maintain a balanced and active playful lifestyle. The development of a lifelong commitment to play is not only possible but highly beneficial for individuals' physical, emotional, and intellectual wellbeing. By pursuing leisure activities that emphasise play, promoting play within social relationships, and overcoming societal and personal barriers, adults can sustain a playful attitude throughout life.

Recommitting to play: For them and for you

As you reach the end of this chapter, I invite you to pause and reflect, not only on the young people you support but on your own relationship with play.

If we are to genuinely support adolescents in developing a lifelong commitment to play, we must be willing to model it. Young people notice far more than what we say: they notice how we move through the world, how we handle stress, how we celebrate, how we rest, and how we relate. When they see adults who are curious, enraptured, creative, and willing to laugh at themselves, they understand that growing older does not have to mean growing stagnant or disconnected. Our playfulness gives them permission to keep theirs.

Ask yourself:

When was the last time you played just for the sake of it?
Do you make room for humour, spontaneity, or creativity in your work with young people or in your own free time?
What would it look like to bring more imaginative, social, physical, or reflective play into your life, not as an extra task but as a way of being?

Perhaps, like Tina Turner's, your moments of happiness come when you are fully immersed, body and soul, in something that lights you up: something that connects you to others, to rhythm, to energy, to presence. That is play. And it is worth protecting. As practitioners, educators, youth workers, and carers, we are in a unique position. We can create environments where play is taken seriously, where it is valued for life. We can challenge the narrative that adulthood must be dry and solemn. And in doing so, we not only offer young people tools for resilience and joy but reclaim them for ourselves. So go full Proud Mary. Not just for them but for you.

References

Barnett, L.A. (2011) 'How playfulness affects mental health and wellbeing in adulthood', *Play and Culture Studies*, 12, pp. 143–158.

Bateson, P. and Martin, P. (2013) *Play, Playfulness, Creativity and Innovation*. Cambridge, UK: Cambridge University Press.

Fancourt, D. and Finn, S. (2019) *What is the Evidence on the Role of the Arts in Improving Health and Well-Being? A Scoping Review*. Copenhagen: WHO Regional Office for Europe.

Granic, I., Lobel, A. and Engels, R.C.M.E. (2014) 'The benefits of playing video games', *American Psychologist*, 69(1), pp. 66–78.

Kaufman, S.B. and Gregoire, C. (2015) *Wired to Create: Unraveling the Mysteries of the Creative Mind*. New York: TarcherPerigee.

Pang, D. and Proyer, R.T. (2018) 'The benefits of being playful: The relationship of playfulness with flow and mindfulness', *Applied Cognitive Psychology*, 32(6), pp. 818–826.

Proyer, R.T. (2014) 'Perceived functions of playfulness in romantic relationships', *Journal of Psychology*, 148(6), pp. 716–735.

Proyer, R.T. (2017) 'A new structural model for adult playfulness: Insights from a multi-sample study', *Journal of Personality*, 85(2), pp. 204–218.

Proyer, R.T., Gander, F., Brauer, K. and Chick, G. (2020) 'Adult playfulness and its relationship with positive psychological functioning', *Current Psychology*, 39(4), pp. 1228–1239.

Proyer, R. T. and Jehle, N. (2013) The basic components of adult playfulness and their relation with personality: The hierarchical factor structure of seventeen instruments. *Personality and Individual Differences*, 55(7), pp. 811–816. doi:10.1016/j.paid.2013.07.010

Ratey, J.J. and Hagerman, E. (2008) *Spark: The Revolutionary New Science of Exercise and the Brain*. New York: Little, Brown.

Richards, R. (2007) *Everyday Creativity and the Healthy Mind: Dynamic New Paths for Self and Society*. New York: American Psychological Association.

Rogers, C., Zhaoyang, R., Lo, S.S. and Smyth, J.M. (2019) 'How brief moments of physical activity improve mood in daily life: A within-person approach', *Health Psychology*, 38(10), pp. 929–937.

Seligman, M.E.P. (2011) *Flourish: A Visionary New Understanding of Happiness and Well-being*. New York: Free Press.

Conclusion

In my first textbook, I researched the happiness index and found myself inspired by Michael J. Fox and his trip to Bhutan in his pursuit to find the happiest place in the world (Cole, 2023). As a child born in the eighties, I have watched *Back to the Future* many times, and I found writing about his work brought back good memories of watching a story that would bring me my own happiness on each viewing. If the first few chords of Huey Lewis and the News' 'The Power of Love' come on, you will find my shoulders going and me reaching for my air guitar. My second book was also influenced in its conclusion by a childhood movie: *The Blues Brothers* (Cole, 2024) brought reflection as to how their journey across Chicago came from a place of love and the need to look with a solution-focused lens. You may see a running theme here: the soundtrack to this movie is still frequently played, I know how to shake a tail feather, and I will point out to the people in the room that 'you, me, them' need someone to love, with a makeshift microphone.

As a reflective practitioner and someone who is informed by evidence-based approaches but also believes in superstitions (if you walk down the pavement with me, you will find me, like I did when I was five years old, sidestepping so as not to walk over three drain covers), I wondered where I could incorporate an influential movie into this book. I quickly knew which one, and it stemmed from a conversation with our eldest daughter shortly after her eighteenth birthday. She had asked me when she was younger if we could get a matching tattoo when she was eighteen, and she was reminding me of the promise. One of my rules in life is to try to say yes more than I say no, in order to open the opportunities that make me and those around me happy. As this decision was a lifetime commitment, though, I asked her to think very carefully of what reminded her of our relationship and would be something that had meaning to both of us. She thought about it and came back with 'dinosaurs'. I had questions.

When my children were younger, we would often seek out places where there was a dinosaur theme. We would learn fun facts about the different species and would make up the front room with pillows, blankets, and snacks to watch reruns of the *Jurassic World* movies. If we drove along a road that

DOI: 10.4324/9781003562368-18

Conclusion   133

Figure 17.1 A photo taken by the author, Fey Cole, of her husband and children at the Lego House dinosaur display in Billund, Denmark.

reminded us of the landscape in the movie, my husband and I would start the 'nah-nah-narrr' soundtrack that opens the films. In fact, when our middle daughter was around six, she went through a stage of responding to us only as a Pterodactyl, defiantly adamant that the noise she made was how they would have sounded, and we went with it until the phase passed. As they grew older, I continued to unconsciously seek out spots where there were dinosaurs, and I still point them out if I notice them, like a parent points out a cow in a field as you pass them on a train. It was not a flower, symbol, or quote that made my daughter think of her childhood and what is special to us. It was a Triceratops that represented us. I was good with that: fun, silliness, some knowledge weaved in, and not taking ourselves too seriously. It was the perfect representation of our connection and love.

This book has been a complicated one to source reams of research for. Play during the adolescent years is so vitally important, but it is a space where researchers have yet to explore in depth. I hope that you have found it a practical and thought-provoking process to read through the chapters and that you have been able to consider the how and why of approaching play with those in their teenage years. It requires us, as the adults, to lead the way and show those we work with that it is ok to be themselves and to explore their dreams, feelings, and relationships through playful mechanisms. Play can be the most powerful catalyst for learning and connects us with the community around us. It makes us feel better and brings us laughter. Why would we not want more play in our lives?

As I have approached the end of this book, spring has sprung and I have given myself time to reconnect with evening walks and more time outdoors to clear my head and catch up with my husband, sharing what we have both been up to during the day. We live close to a large park where you can choose to walk around the lake, the sports fields, or the more secluded woodland area. Some days, we get round all three, sometimes we wander around one of the paths, but on each of our evenings this week, we have seen a substantial group of teenagers approaching from a distance, dressed in hoodies, taking up the path. As they approach, they scatter sideways to open up the path for us, one bends down to give our dog Scruffy a scratch behind the ear, one greets me with a 'Hello Mrs Cole', one responds that there is 'no craic' as a response to me asking what the craic is, one asks me what we have for tea later and tells me what time he will be home. From a distance, they can look like a daunting crowd to meet, especially on the quieter back paths. To me, they are the little boys I have known for many years, with one of them my darling baby (something I would refrain from sharing as our paths cross in front of his mates!), who I know would willingly give a hand if they met someone on their travels in need. As I wander on, I notice there is no official space for them in this large park. They might look mischievous going down to the children's swings or finding a stick that ends up rattling against the fence as they walk. I am not the only one they greet as they wander. They nod their head or say hello as they pass strangers, there is no malice in their journey, the teens are just spending time together and making use of one of the only open spaces that is somewhat open for them to be in. As you transition away from reading this book (which I hope you return to as you progress in your path of play), look around at the environment. Not just the classroom or the youth setting you work in directly, but look beyond this, the corridors, the local community spaces, the bus stops, the shopping centres, the town centre. Are they really accessible for teenagers? Do they allow for fun, social time, conversations? Do they segregate the teens from the rest of society or allow for different age groups to fully utilise them together? Every time we make a space more inclusive and open for playful interactions, we build a stronger, happier, and more cohesive community.

References

Cole, F. (2023) *Intergenerational Practice in Schools and Settings*. Abingdon: Routledge.
Cole, F. (2024) *An Educator's Guide to Project-Based Learning: Turning Theory into Practice*. London: Routledge (David Fulton Publishers).

Index

Africa 69, 89, 107
Ahmed, Sara 43
artificial intelligence 47, 65–66, 97
Al Jalila Foundation 49–50
Arctic 108
Aristotle 51–52
Australia 54, 107–108

Bailey, R. 36–37
Barnes, J. 52
Barnett, L.A. 125
Barron et al. 47
Bartlett, Steven 59–60
Bateson & Martin 60, 68, 128
Bavelier et al. 44
Bhutan 132
Blackledge, Sinead 61
Blakemore & Centers 66
Blakemore & Choudhury 10
Blakemore & Mills 8, 12
Blumer, H. 86
Blurton Jones, H. 69
Bolivia 65–66
Boyd, D. 19
Brazil 105
Bronfenbrenner, Urie 84–86, 126
Brown, Brené 18
Brown, Stuart 14
Bukowski, W.M. 13
Burnett et al. 9
Burridge, K.O.L. 69

Canada 94–95
Casey et al. 9
Chao & Tseng 106
China 71–72, 105–106, 112, 118
Choi et al. 68
Chudacoff, H.P. 43, 65

Classcraft 94–95, 99
Cohen, S. 53
Cole, Fey 14, 20–21, 25, 40, 132–134
Commission on Adult Vocational Teaching and Learning (CAVTL) Principles 72
Confucius 51
Craft, A. 27, 47
Crone & Dahl 9
Csikszentmihalyi, Mihaly 1, 20–21, 60, 75–76, 121

Dahlgren & Szczepanski 113
Danko & Greene 122
Deci & Ryan 15
Delhi 54
Denmark 36–37, 44, 68
Department of Health & Social Care 118
Deterding et al. 73
Dewey, John 38–40, 42–44, 52
Diamond & Lee 79
Diamond & Ling 8–9
Diaz & Estoque-Lonez 95, 99
Dillon et al. 86
drama 17, 27, 34, 46–47, 75–76, 120–121
Dubai 49–51
Dweck 33–34

Ecclestone & Hayes 49
Ecological Systems Theory 84–86
Education DataLab 32
Edwards et al. 66
Elkind, D. 10
Ellsworth, E. 53
England 61, 67, 80–81, 93, 103
Eriksen, Erik 18–19, 74

Ethiopia 110
experiential learning 9, 14, 38–39, 42–43, 58, 73–74, 107, 120

failure 17, 28, 33, 41, 46–47, 50, 59–60, 79–80, 87, 122–123, 127
Fancourt & Finn 127
feminism/feminist 42–43, 109
Finland 34, 43–44, 46, 54, 95–96, 105
Fisher, E.P. 78
Fisher Act 5–6
Flip 96
Flourish Agenda 49
Flow, Theory of 1, 5, 20–21, 60, 75–76, 121
Fox, Michael J. 133
Fredricks & Simpkins 105
Fredrickson, B.L. 33
Freire, Paolo 53, 74
Freizeit 34
Friluftsliv 104, 112–113

Gadotti, M. 53
Garrison, J. 52
Gee, James Paul 95
gender 20–21, 42–43, 53, 66–67, 108–109, 116
Germany 34, 52, 113
Gielen et al. 94
Gilman, Huebner & Laughlin 115–116
Globalisation 105
Global Education Reform Movement (GERM) 54
Gonku, Mistry & Mosier 106
Gornick & Meyers 68
Granic et al. 12, 130
Gray, Peter 50, 103
Grünke & Cavendish 34
Gu & Wang 72

Haidt, J. 36
Hamari et al. 93–94
Hattie, Professor John 79
Hietala, A. 122
Himba 109
Holmes et al. 97
Hong Kong 120
hooks, bell 42–43, 53
Howard-Jones, P. 10, 14
Huang & Spector 97
Hughes, Bob 101–102
Huizinga, J. 73
Hyttinen, T. 66

India 52, 54, 105
intergenerational 85, 87, 106–107, 109–110, 112
Italy 52

Jamaica 84
Jansz et al. 20
Japan 24, 33, 68, 99, 104, 113, 121
Jarvis, Newman & Swiniarski 62
JoyFE 61
Ju/'hoansi 69

Kahoot! 92–93, 99
Kane, M.J. 12
Kangas, M. 46
Kapp, Karl 98
Kapur, M. 47
Kaufman & Gregoire 128
Kaye et al. 44
Kim, S. 68
Kolb et al. 11, 58
Korczak, Janusz 53
Kozulin, A. 53

Lahtero & Risku 34
Latin America 53
LEGO 44, 58, 65, 122–123
leisure 11, 13, 40, 43, 62, 65–69, 104, 108, 128–130
Leone et al. 73
Lester & Russell 11, 71–73, 103
Li et al. 98
Lillard et al. 79
Lonka et al. 44
Luckin, R. 47
Luna et al. 9

Maasai 89–90
Mahoney, Cairns & Farmer 114–115
Marwick & Boyd 19
McRobbie, Angela 43
Mezirow, J. 41
mind-mapping 30
Minecraft 93, 95–96, 99
Minimally Invasive Education (MIE) 54–55
Mintz, S. 65
Mistake Wall 60
Mitra, Sugata 54
Mongolia 108
Montessori, Maria 52
Mukherjee, M. 52
music 11–12, 28, 34–35, 49, 52, 61, 87–88, 90, 107, 121, 125–129

Namibia 109
nature 22, 52, 104, 112, 123
Netherlands 36, 94
Nigeria 104
Nishida, Kitaro 24
Nonaka, Ikujiro 24–25
Northern Ireland 61, 67, 80, 96, 99
Norway 43, 104

Olympics 67
outdoors/parks 21, 36, 61, 66, 86–90, 112, 134

Pang & Proyer 126
Panksepp, Jaak 10, 15
Papua New Guinea 67, 90
Paris 67
Paus et al. 8
Pellegrini, A.L. 10–11, 58, 66
Pellegrini & Smith 9, 33
Peppler & Bender 121
phone-based childhood 36–37
Piaget, Jean 14, 67–68
Pomerantz & Raby 20
project-based learning (PBL) 14, 17, 20–21, 30, 39, 46, 58, 66, 71–72, 75, 120
Proyer & Jehle 126
Proyer et al. 125–126, 129

Ramani & Siegler 96
Ratey, J.J. 36
Ratey & Hagerman 127
Reggio Emilia approach 66
Renold, E. 109
Resnick, M. 47, 50
Reyes-Garcia et al. 65
Richards, R. 126
Rizvi & Lingard 54
Robinson, Sir Ken 41–42, 46–47, 54
Rogers et al. 128
Rogoff, B. 40
role-modelling 3, 34, 62, 115, 118
Romeo, R.D. 10
Russia 53

Sahlberg, Pasi 44, 46, 54
Samoa 109
Samuelsson & Carlsson 86
San 107
Self-Determination Theory 15, 32
Seligman, M.E.P. 129

Selwyn, N. 47
Shaw, George Bernard 8
Singapore 118
Singh et al. 43
Sky Sports 67
Slattery et al. 95
social media 5–6, 19, 36, 75, 104–105
South America 69
South Korea 33, 68, 94, 99, 105, 118, 121
Spencer et al. 9
Steinberg, L. 12–13
Steinberg & Morris 19
Sturrock & Else 115
Sun & Rao 72
Suri 110
Sutton-Smith, B. 13, 34, 50, 57, 59, 71
Sweden 68, 86, 112
Symbolic Interactionism 87

Tagore, Rabindranath 52
Thomas & Brown 47
Thompson, E.P. 68
Tomporowski et al. 118
Treblinka 53
Trobriand Islands 90
Tsimane 65
Turkle, S. 18

UN Environment Programme 98
United Kingdom 21, 27, 34, 41, 61, 66–67, 86, 93
United Nations Convention on the Rights of the Child (UNCRC) 13, 53, 62
Universal Design for Learning (UDL) 97
USSR 53

Visva-Bharati University 52
Vygotsky, Lev 8–9, 14, 40–41, 52–53, 58, 73

Wales 34, 102
Weisner, T.S. 69
Women's World Cup 67
Wood & Eagly 67
World Economic Forum 47

Yanomami 108
Yousafzai & Lamb 55

Zarrett et al. 120

For Product Safety Concerns and Information please contact our EU
representative GPSR@taylorandfrancis.com
Taylor & Francis Verlag GmbH, Kaufingerstraße 24, 80331 München, Germany

www.ingramcontent.com/pod-product-compliance
Lightning Source LLC
Chambersburg PA
CBHW051543230426
43669CB00015B/2702